MW01156585

"Patrick Paul C
human journey of spiritual awakening entails. He has a gift—not only in relaying words, concepts and experiences but also through his heartfelt vulnerability and compassionate presence toward the service of humanity. In his new book, *Endless Awakening*, Patrick Paul Garlinger is a humble master, expressing a level of truth-telling that leaves the ego speechless and initiates the awakening to freedom your Spirit has longed for. All of Patrick's books are treasures; this one definitely belongs in your treasure chest!"
— SIMRAN, award-winning author and founding publisher of *11:11 Magazine*

"I love Patrick Paul Garlinger's *Endless Awakening*. The flowing, easy-to-read, and intimate conversational style easily guides us across many intricate healing models. The author's share of his own traumas, emotions, and recovery gives us a perfect understanding of the shamanic and spiritual processes. It also gives us a solid holding hand to accept our own unique journey. This book is a true gem, and its time has come for those who heed the inner call for transformation." — Itzhak Beery, author of *The Gift of Shamanism*, *Shamanic Transformations*, and *Shamanic Healing*, founder and publisher of shamanportal.org / www.itzhakbeery.com

"This book lives up to its title by awakening you, again and again, to deep insights and profound, new ways of seeing things. Patrick peels back the layers of complex topics like time, emotions, and memory with such accessibility and clarity—it is like having a trusted friend explain life's truths to you in ways that allow you to follow along and apply it all to your own experience. This book will inspire and energize you and open your eyes to the magic that is within and around you at all times." — Yael Shy, author of *What Now? Meditation for Your Twenties and Beyond* and CEO of Mindfulness Consulting, LLC

"*Endless Awakening* is a practical guide to consciousness written by a natural teacher. I had the uncanny experience, as I read, that he was standing alongside me as the stories, principles, lessons and healings unfolded, taking my hand and gently guiding me to a gentler home within myself. These are words that create change." — Jacqueline Freeman, author of *Song of Increase* and *What Bees Want*, and publisher of www.spiritbee.com

ENDLESS
AWAKENING

TIME,

PARADOX,

AND THE PATH TO

ENLIGHTENMENT

PATRICK PAUL GARLINGER

Jerriannah,
May you find peace of mind
in the paradoxes of time,
Patrick

Red Elixir
Rhinebeck, New York

Paperback ISBN: 978-1-954744-81-3
eBook ISBN: 978-1-954744-82-0

Library of Congress Control Number: 978-1-954744-83-7

Book and cover design by Colin Rolfe

Red Elixir is an imprint of Monkfish Book Publishing Company

Red Elixir
22 East Market Street, Suite 304
Rhinebeck, NY 12572
(845) 876-4861
monkfishpublishing.com

CONTENTS

INTRODUCTION

⫘

MY CLIENT STROLLED in, beaming and happy. Their outward appearance did not betray any pain or need for spiritual
guidance.[1] After an initial exchange of pleasantries, I tuned in
and felt a deep sadness wash over me. I then saw the image
of a young child, crying out desperately for attention. My eyes
watered, and I shared what I was feeling.

"Really? I already healed this."

"It feels like this young child is still there. Can you tell me
what happened?" I asked.

My client went on to describe an enormously painful
childhood trauma but reassured me that years of work had
already healed this pain. I reiterated what I perceived—that
this younger version was still there, asking to be held and seen.
Some months later, we reconnected, and my client shared that
after our session, the childhood pain had resurfaced fully. After
months of dedicated inner work, the weight of that trauma had
lifted.

As an intuitive, I encounter a version of this story time and
again. The details change, but the structure is almost always the
same. It is the story of awakening to one's pain and engaging
in various healing practices to feel whole again. The pain is not
always childhood trauma. Other versions take the form of not

knowing one's purpose or struggling with a sense of belonging in the world. The pain might also appear more broadly as a deep dissatisfaction with life and a sense that there's more to be seen than what our conventional, modern world has to offer us. In each of these instances, the seeker awakens and, after some time, believes that they have uncovered their true selves, healed their wounds, or arrived at their coveted destination. Then they hit an impasse, or the pain they thought healed returns.

It can be distressing to discover that the journey is not over. The difficult news I must impart is that the journey—what you think of as a healing journey or path to wholeness—is never over. Instead, the path to healing is to relinquish what you think of as the spiritual journey altogether.

The journey usually begins with what is commonly called an awakening. A spiritual awakening occurs when you realize that what you feel and perceive is not the whole of life. You start asking questions like: What is the meaning of life? Is there a higher power of some kind? Even when we contemplate those lofty questions, we end up coming back to three very basic ones: Who am I? Why am I here? How do I feel whole again? Underlying these questions is a feeling of discontent. The reason we awaken and embark on a spiritual journey is because we feel like something is not quite right in our lives, or something is missing. We want to feel whole, loved, and alive. We feel that there's more to life than the humdrum of eating, sleeping, and working. We feel that we are here for a purpose, even if we don't quite know what it is, and we want to feel loved and connected with the world.

As you unravel these metaphysical questions, you discover that life is not all that our physical senses tell us, nor what our conventional ways of thinking and talking say about the nature of reality. You might discover through meditation that your thoughts are not always true or real. You might pursue different states of consciousness through plant medicine or psychedelics. Perhaps you have an out-of-body or energetic experience of some kind. You might start to learn new concepts, like how our categories of identity seem natural or necessary but are constructions, or like the importance of gratitude and forgiveness in shaping your attitude to life. You realize, in short, that your language and perception of the world is a partial and distorted vision of what is possible. You might even start to wonder if the world that you see, yourself included, is a grand illusion.

Your awakening might be rooted in Buddhist thought or New Age spirituality or some other tradition. You might think of your true self as presence or awareness or believe that you have a soul and are a divine being. Whatever your tradition and the vocabulary you use, you intuit that you don't have to suffer or feel incomplete, that somehow your natural state is one of peace and love, where you don't feel dissatisfied with life or a profound well of lack at your core. You also realize that your ego, the part of you that has been steering your life until now, needs to be modified, expanded, or healed in some way. Once you realize that life can be different from what you've experienced thus far, you embark wholeheartedly on a journey of tending to your ego and its wounds.

If this describes your path, then you are in the right place. You have already learned some combination of wisdom and practices—whether meditation, yoga, mantra, plant medicine, tarot, reiki, astrology, or some other methodology—and you're making emotional and spiritual progress while continuing to deepen your knowledge. But, somehow, the state that you thought you'd reach, a place of unconditional love or peace, still eludes you. You find yourself falling into the same patterns. The childhood wound you thought would heal still triggers you.

Perhaps you pick up a new book or modality of healing, hoping that this is the piece you've been missing. You abandon one form of meditation for another. You try tapping or angelic healing. You reach out to a shaman, a psychic medium, or another energy healer, hoping that this person will help you reach this elusive state of being. You read every article about what you've been doing wrong with manifestation and why you can't attract the life you desire. You believe that you are missing something, some piece of information or wisdom, some tool or technique, that will finally unlock what you know to be true—that the answers, and the divine, are already inside.

Here's the rub: The very idea of a spiritual path can be misleading. When we think of ourselves on a path or journey, we develop a sense of a trajectory that in time will lead to an arrival at a destination. That destination goes by many names: Enlightenment, transcendence, wholeness, and ascension are just a few. The fundamental problem with this approach is that your mind understands the journey in a particular way. You perceive spirituality in a linear sense as moving from a state of ego slumber to awakening, and then to some final state— transcendence or enlightenment. Within that framework, you chart a linear timeline, leaving behind the darkness and moving above to a new, higher level. There is a trajectory, around time and discrete stages, built into your model of spirituality. When you see the path this way, you fall prey to an older form of consciousness that, paradoxically, keeps you from experiencing the wholeness you seek.

Part of the problem lies in how spiritual wisdom now circulates. The more social media and the internet have become the repositories for spiritual guidance, the less radical and challenging spiritual wisdom has become. Wisdom gets reduced to easily digestible memes. Heart-felt proclamations of "love and light" and overly simplified principles, stripped of nuance, spread with ease. Living through spiritual inspiration on social media, most seekers have not yet committed themselves to the deep work of uprooting the basic underlying structures of thought that give rise to their suffering. The wisdom they received early on about their vibrational frequency or the fifth dimension, which initially gave them a new perspective on life, holds them back from experiencing a deeper sense of peace.

After you awaken and experience some spiritual growth, the deepest structures of your mind still mold your perception of reality. At the most fundamental level, the mind creates itself as a separate entity in time and space, a discrete material being separate from the fabric of space and time. The linear, logical mind must give up its attachment to that way of understanding. It must release its conventional understanding of time and embrace a series of paradoxes: You are always healing yet already whole. You are one with everyone yet an autonomous being. You are innately connected to the divine, yet you are also a material being in the world. Transcendence feels like it will be found out there, in the future, at some other point, because you are not feeling transcendent now, *and* you are already transcendent, already whole, already enlightened. This is the fundamental paradox: How can I be whole and broken, awake and asleep, *at the same time?*

There is no greater paradox for our lives than the paradox of time. In fact, the paradoxes of time and spirituality are one and the same. To move beyond the feeling of being stuck that so many seekers experience, we must develop our awareness of how our minds construct time—dividing the world into past, present, and future. Very often, when confronted with this feeling of being stuck, where we cannot escape the pain of our past or the fear of a future where we never feel healed, we may feel a desire to escape this material world altogether as a way to escape the present. You might focus exclusively on connecting with spirit, with the unseen world beyond this one. When you view spirituality as an escape from duality, it becomes another trap of the ego. That is how our constructed minds keep us from transcendence. At some point while doing our spiritual practices, we come to realize that illumination or enlightenment is not a state attained at some future point or by hiding from this world. It is a dimension of experience available to us now, yet paradoxically, we might not experience enlightenment until some moment in the future. We must embrace the paradox.

Much of the spiritual wisdom you've learned until now has given you a false sense of trajectory. The truth is that the wily ego often sneaks its way through the back door: You start to believe you're failing if you're not feeling blissfully happy all the time, so you begin to practice toxic positivity. You start to believe you're being dragged down by others, so instead of seeing the divine in them, you embrace a spiritual identity in which you go looking for your community and reject anyone who doesn't share your beliefs. You start to see this world as flawed, where true spirituality cannot flourish, and dismiss reality as an illusion, or you hold fast to the idea that a new Earth, enlightened and perfect, is just around the corner. In other words, you fall back into division, judgment, and rejection—the hallmarks of the negative ego. You divide yourself from the world in time and space, seeking to be elsewhere and at some other point in time, a future where life is better. These older forms of consciousness, rooted in time and trajectory, often still operate beneath all of the proclamations of "love and light" or "high vibe."

The path of spiritual mastery involves reshaping your mind's perception of time as the principal way that we understand our reality so as to embrace paradox and circularity over linear and binary ways of thinking. That is no easy task, because much of your mind was formed around these ways of thinking and those structures of thought have been reinforced for many years. These deeply ingrained habits of thought and ways of seeing the world limit our perception. The truth is that we never arrive, yet we are already home. Yet how can we be home when our lives feel so incomplete? We must embrace contradiction, paradox, and competing truths to break through the limited ways our minds construct our world. Those contradictions and paradoxes inevitably come back to our understanding of time. Indeed, our very existence as immortal spirit in a mortal frame means that we are an embodiment of paradox. We are timelessness bound by time. We are God trapped in an hourglass.

* * *

In my time as an intuitive working with others and as an author, there has been considerable movement away from gurus and figures of authority to the idea that each of us has a direct connection to the divine. This is a powerful and potent truth. Nevertheless, we misunderstand that truth and reinforce our egos when we believe that no one else has anything to teach us. You can eschew all gurus and still benefit from assistance from others; the answers may be inside, but you may need help from others to unlock them. The notion that you have nothing to learn from anybody else because "the divine is inside" and we're all connected to spirit is one example of how an older consciousness gets replicated within a spiritual truth. If you believe that you are the sole source of wisdom, it's likely that your negative ego is twisting that spiritual principle to reinforce its sense of superiority.

This book serves as a guide and offers you insights to

deepen your spiritual work. Its teachings are derived from multiple sources. My experiences in higher consciousness and with plant medicine are the main ones.[2] I also draw on my experiences using my psychic faculties to assist others with their own emotional and karmic blocks. Where appropriate, I've included references to other works of spiritual wisdom, physics, and cultural theory. Spiritual wisdom should be in dialogue with other domains of thought. Sometimes I draw on science fiction or popular culture; there's no need for spirituality to pretend to be so rarefied or otherworldly.

The book takes you on a survey of key aspects of life—emotions, the body, our awareness of time, spiritual energy, identity and the changing nature of the self, relationships, our capacity to trust life, and death. Each chapter offers a new perspective, rooted in time and paradox, to help you broaden your conventional way of relating to that area of life. At each moment, your consciousness, built on an edifice of beliefs and experiences, creates the world you perceive. That includes how you interpret spiritual wisdom. So how do you alter your consciousness to perceive your reality differently?

The impasse is the path. Every limitation or block is the way forward. The obstacle that you perceive as keeping you from wholeness is the portal to that wholeness. You transcend your limits by accepting that you have limits. You grow by letting go of the idea that you need to grow. You arrive by letting go of the desire to arrive. Ultimately, you no longer see your journey in linear time, as stages of growth from asleep to awake to transcended, because that understanding of enlightenment is the main limitation of the human ego. Instead, you see that your very perception of time is both the barrier and the portal through which to connect with the divine. You transcend time by accepting that time structures your entire life and yet time is a paradox that we cannot solve. Once you understand that your awakening is without end, you will have fully awakened.

EMOTIONS:
YOUR PAIN IS A PORTAL

ONE OF MY earliest and most painful memories is of a schoolyard encounter in the first grade. My family had moved to Utah, and I was ignorant of religious differences. I had been baptized Catholic, and my peers were mostly Mormon, which meant little to me as a six-year-old. My memory begins with feeling hurt that the other kids wouldn't play with me during recess. I confronted the teacher. "Why won't you play with Patrick?" she asked three of my classmates who were standing nearby. One of them whispered, as if saying something sinful, "He's Catholic!" The teacher looked at me with pity and uttered, "It's not his fault." My cheeks flushed with shame, as if she had identified some flaw in me that was beyond redemption.

In response, I retaliated. It was not me who was flawed, but God. Afterward I refused to go to catechism or church, and God no longer had any meaning for me. I saw God as a source of division created by humans to justify their actions. From then on, I responded to any mention of religion or spirituality with derision. The emotional weight of that single episode shaped my relationship to spirituality until I was in my late thirties. I not only spurned God, but I also kept people at arm's length, having learned that differences in spiritual beliefs could lead to rejection and shame.

I am hardly alone in this pattern. Even if the details differ for you, all of us have rooms of pain tightly packed with the remains of the past. We carry around old wounds, abandoned dreams, paths not taken now shellacked with regret, and trauma or abuse for which we had no defenses. This is the shadow side of our being. In response to this human condition, we often bury our pain, persuading ourselves that we have moved past the hurt. Every so often, a door to one of those back rooms in our minds opens ever so slightly, offering us a glimpse of the detritus of our lives. Our tendency is to slam the door shut and further buttress it with another deadbolt of repression. We excel at burial, not realizing that we are suffocating ourselves in the process.

One of the primary ways that we bury our pain is by turning to pleasure. We run away from discomfort and pursue entertainment. Drugs, food, sex, the internet, and other forms of pleasure become antidotes to our pain, which offer only temporary relief. If we are not successful in suppressing or numbing the pain, we tend to externalize it. Outrage and reactivity come easily, as if we were a hot coal ready to catch fire with a dash of igniter fluid in the form of a small word of criticism or a judgmental glance. We become drama queens, ready to claw out the eyes of the next careless interlocutor.

Paradoxically, the more we exert ourselves in trying to get rid of or away from our pain, the greater it grows. Pushing away emotions never works. These feelings are pieces of you clamoring for your attention. They might subside for a bit, but they will be triggered once again in the future. Suppressing your emotions only confirms that they, not you, are in the driver's seat of your life. Trying to avoid the discomforting sensations fluctuating through your mind and body is itself an emotional response.

But there's a different way to relate to your pain, neither numbing it nor projecting it onto others. It's so simple that it might even seem laughable: To heal your pain, you must feel your pain. The simplicity of this process does not mean that it is easy. In fact, as tautological as it may sound, feeling into our emotional wounds is *painful*. But when you learn to embrace your pain, meeting it wholeheartedly and with compassion, it becomes a portal to something far greater than you could have imagined: You discover that your brightest light resides deep inside there, not in some heavenly realm beyond your reach. It is then that you realize that your perception of yourself as broken or wounded is the real wound that you need to release. It is the story of being hurt, in the past, with your healing deferred to the future, that you must shed to find true peace.

THE POWER OF ACCEPTANCE

On the fifth day of a nine-day silent meditation retreat, I woke up at 2:00 a.m. filled with terror. Flashing through my mind were the scariest scenes from films that I had seen as a kid: *The Amityville Horror, The Exorcist, The Omen, Poltergeist,* and *Salem's Lot*. Demons, ghosts, vampires, and other kinds of malevolent entities, and a ton of creepy music, were cascading through my brain, eliciting the most intense fear I've ever felt in my life.

These films had given me all sorts of nightmares as a child, and the fear they inspired was the flip side of my rejection of God; God had rejected me too, and therefore I was certain to be preyed upon by emissaries of the damned. As an adult, I didn't walk around consciously afraid, as if the mere mention of one of them might send me into a panic, but I didn't enjoy horror movies and found myself avoiding them.

The depth of my childhood fear was revealed at this retreat. Panic-stricken, my heart was racing, and I was gulping for air. Sweat gushed from every pore, soaking my clothes. The fear was itchy, almost electric, like a current running through my body, especially my skin. Each time my mind scrolled through the images and my body squeezed out another bucket of sweat, the fear diminished slightly. I remained steadfast and allowed that fear to wash over me instead of trying to push it away or calm myself down.

Over two hours later, the images, fear, and sweat all subsided. I exchanged my drenched T-shirt for a dry one and fell into a deep sleep. The rest of the meditation retreat passed without incident. By diving into the pain, I was able to heal this childhood fear.

It was not my first experience of this kind. Years before, in Sedona, Arizona, I worked with a shamanic practitioner who led me through a process known as "soul retrieval." The idea is that when we experience a traumatic episode, a part of our essence splinters and leaves us.[1] We heal when that part can be recovered and reintegrated into our sense of self. As the practitioner began the soul retrieval, a profound well of grief and loneliness welled up in me, and I sobbed wildly as he connected with this sense of despair that I had carried around. It was a core feeling that I did not belong on this planet and was an outsider in so many social interactions. The next day, I stood in the desert and railed at God for sending me back here, again and again. As with my supernatural fears, the relief I felt in touching this pain so deeply was profound. Sadness, then anger, and more sadness, poured out of me until I was empty.

This is the power of accepting your emotions so completely that they resolve on their own.

* * *

To accept your emotions, you first need to repair your understanding of them. Those of us who resist feeling them need to stop seeing our emotions as an enemy to be vanquished. Many of us learn at an early age that our emotions, particularly unbridled expressions of them, are irrational surges of energy that need to be quelled. Boys are often taught to suppress their emotions at an early age; somehow, certain emotions, like sadness or vulnerability, are seen as flaws to be eradicated. But the cultural norms around emotions extend to all of us—we are taught that being emotional is somehow a sign of failure or weakness. Any negative perception you have for your emotions or the emotions of others needs to be released. Emotions are part of being human.

For years, like many men, I thought that stoicism was my path to liberation. I honed my flight skills, so much so that if there were certifications in emotional flight, I'd be a star pilot. I regarded my schoolteachers, many of whom were men, who seemed peaceful and in control of their emotions, as superior to those who couldn't keep them in check. I assumed from these role models' staid appearance that they had conquered their emotions by pushing them aside or driving them into submission. Not that I was actually stoic; I felt my emotions deeply. But I learned to hide them, maintaining the appearance of neutrality. Of course, years later I would realize my mind had room after room stuffed with unresolved emotions, like a Marie Kondo nightmare.

Repairing your relationship to your emotions means accepting that they are a language—the language of sensation, spoken in and through the body. Put differently, emotions are *information*. As Kahlil Gibran says, "Your pain is the breaking of the shell that encloses your understanding."[2] As information, emotions tell us how connected we feel to the world. Love, peace, compassion, and joy reflect our sense of unity with the world that surrounds us. Anger, fear, sadness, and shame tend to isolate or separate us from the world, telling us that we now stand in opposition to it.

Some of our most painful emotions are fear, anger, and rejection. Fear is almost always tied to the future, to a perception based on prior moments from our past where we endured some loss of security or power and felt threatened. Fear attempts to offer a prediction that says that if you say or do something, the consequences will be terrible. Anger is related to fear in that it is the feeling we project onto the person or event that has triggered a loss of security or power. Anger emerges when we feel powerless, when boundaries have been crossed, and we are made to feel small; anger is the energy that rejects this and tries to regain power. It masks our fear. Finally, feeling unloved or rejected is what creates a desire in us to seek out approval, attention, and affection, to fill the void. This desire is tied to rejection or abandonment.

Pain is the call of the past. These emotions are rooted in past moments where the words and actions of someone hurt us, leaving us insecure about our place in the world. The problem is not that we experience painful emotions. It's that we don't know how to be with painful emotions. Negative emotions are transcribed as memory in our minds and as pain in the tissues of our bodies. We have vivid memories of events in our lives that we experienced as moments of rejection, failure, loss, or trauma. The pain is wired into our bodies and minds in ways that emotionally tepid events are not, which is why you so easily forget what you had for lunch last Tuesday, but not the withering remark from your mother when you were nine.

When we accept that our emotions are information about our past, not our enemies, pain and reactivity become a treasure map to healing. To access that information, you must listen to the language of emotions by feeling the sensations, accompanied by memories and images, as they ripple through the body. This process goes by many names and takes different forms. New Age seekers might call it soul realignment or healing the shadow. Shamans might call it soul retrieval. Psychologists might refer to it as healing the inner child, whom you are learning to reparent. This is the process of retrieving and healing the parts of us that remain hidden, beneath your placid exterior, or that you foist upon others in a never-ending cycle of drama.

Your emotions are pieces of you from a lost time. We learn to recover those bits of ourselves by traveling with our emotions back in time, learning to see how we interpreted past events in our lives. When we see our emotions this way, we can start to journey with our pain to the moments when it was installed deep within us, to those back rooms that we typically like to keep locked up tight.

*　*　*

What are you feeling right in this moment as you contemplate these words? For some, the very mention of feeling your emotional pain is enough to inspire anxiety. We resist our emotions because we fear that we will be drowned by our pain, or we worry that our emotions will demand that we face parts of our lives we would like to avoid. Some of you may sense that acknowledging your feelings would require you to make a radical change in your life, like admitting that you hate your job, or that you no longer love your spouse, or that someone you think of as a friend really isn't one.

Whether it's sadness, anger, despair, anxiety, or some other painful emotion, the emotion becomes worse the more you push it away. Only when you take the risk that your pain will swallow you whole will you realize that it is by feeling that pain fully, without resistance, that you can tread water. *Resistance* to emotion is what drowns you; accepting and allowing the sensations to flow through you becomes a form of life raft. Much of the pain you feel comes when you don't give your pain permission to move through you. You are at war with yourself, but the pain diminishes the more you release the resistance and allow it in.

If you pause and feel into yourself right now, you might notice just how many emotions are percolating beneath your seemingly placid surface. You might feel a bit of boredom, maybe some anticipation, a yearning for more, a hunger for something else, a flash of annoyance. Like all human beings, you are churning with feelings. You fluctuate, from moment to moment, moving from one emotion to the next, often almost imperceptibly. When you slow down and learn to feel your emotions, with all of their depth and subtlety, you can begin to perceive those fluctuations and remain with them.

When you start to feel some kind of painful emotion arise—like sadness, anger, frustration, regret, disappointment, or fear—notice if it shows up in a particular place in the body, if it's in a particular location or across the skin, if it has a texture or a temperature. Paint a picture of that feeling. When we have not practiced feeling our emotions, we very quickly speak in thoughts. We turn to criticism, justification, analysis, or some kind of intellectual response. The machinery of our mind that we've honed over years kicks into gear to process and package the feeling in a way that is far more amenable to us. Without practice, raw emotion can be challenging; we often prefer a more synthesized, artificial, and conceptualized version of our feelings.

Stay with the pain—the sadness, bitterness, anger, outrage—and allow it to flood you, without reacting to it or allowing it to lead you to speak or take action. Breathe and relax. Soften into it. Notice each instance where you want to pull away and feel something else. Instead, feel the resistance. Feel your resistance to feeling resistance. Resistance is a way of measuring the gap between what your emotion is asking of you and how you're responding. The emotion wants to move through your body, and you're attempting to block it. Allow it to wash over you. Continue to feel it, again and again, noticing the subtle efforts to push it away, and then softening and allowing the emotion and your resistance to be there. The practice is a constant tightening and softening, one after the other. In time, the emotion will dissipate.

Developing your capacity to feel that discomfort—to overcome your resistance and stay with negative feelings—is one of the most important steps on a spiritual path. Your goal here is not to feel comfortable. The lesson is, paradoxically, to become comfortable with feeling discomfort. Meeting your emotions with openness, love, and compassion can often allow them to resolve on their own. Hold them lovingly, without a secret desire for them to leave, and they leave on their own. Tell them to leave, and they hide, only to return later like an unwanted houseguest or pesky sibling.

This is, in essence, the practice of meditation. You might think of meditation as sitting on a cushion and holding a certain pose. Those are the external elements. You might think meditation is paying attention to your breath, but that's one technique to practice keeping your attention in one place. In this case, the practice is simply to be with your feelings as they arise. It's also known as *vipassana*.

You might object and say that this is a dangerous approach for someone dealing with profound trauma like abuse. I would agree. For those dealing with rape, emotional or physical abuse, or witnessing a violent death, to name just a few relevant scenarios, this work requires the skilled guidance of a counselor or therapist, someone who can allow you to touch that trauma gingerly and with caution, so as not to retraumatize you.

Spiritual seekers now apply the word *trauma* quite frequently to emotional pain. Some might say that doing so diminishes its specificity for certain kinds of wounds. Nevertheless, trauma work has taught us that most of us are carrying around more wounds than we thought we were, making it clear that deep pain is almost ordinary. It has also taught us that our emotions are embedded in our bodies. In a sense, then, most of us are grappling with some level of trauma, even if we are not dealing with emotional or physical abuse, the kinds of violence to which that term is usually applied. In this way, trauma work shows us that the work of releasing even the most seemingly trivial cut is not unlike the work of dealing with major wounds.

Most of our emotional strife involves the accumulation of different kinds of pain: rejection, disappointment, disempowerment, abandonment, lack, loneliness, hunger, craving, or anger. The sources of emotional pain range from disputes with a spouse or coworker or dealing with neighbors—to getting sick, learning that a parent is dying, or losing your job. You are a rollercoaster of emotions, a teeming mass of unresolved pain accumulated from moment to moment, year to year, from the minutiae of daily interactions and the eruption of serious life events. Your pain, which might not rise to the level of trauma as it has been traditionally defined, might be tied to your first childhood love or unrequited crush, to the ways your mother or father would chastise or punish you, to moments of failure or rejection in school. It might be as small as a bunch of schoolkids refusing to play with you because you don't share the same religion, or a deep fright from watching scary movies, or the pain of feeling like something is wrong with you because your father left when you were ten years old. Your pain might be more systemic, like believing that you do not belong in this world because of your race, sexual orientation, gender identification, or some other part of you that feels rejected by society.

For those who have lived their entire lives in pain, being told that you need to feel your pain until it resolves can be an overwhelming suggestion. Sometimes we need respite, comfort, and solace. You need to know that there is a way to live a life filled with joy, wonder, and comfort. You need to restore your faith in life when loss and conflict have worn you down. This is the path of self-care and self-love, where you learn to give yourself the kind of comfort and support that you have been denied. This is a necessary antidote to stress and anxiety, with its deeply pernicious effects on the mind and body. You have spent your life managing your pain, and now you are learning to relate to it without resistance, without pushing it away. This means that you also learn to be gentle with yourself and step back from the process at times. Guidance from a qualified meditation teacher can be enormously helpful in this regard.

You might also object, quite logically, that the directive to "just feel it" might sound perfectly reasonable, a sort of spiritual slogan inspired by Nike. But for those of you who have spent your lives honing your skills of repression, you might find that accessing your feelings seems almost impossible. Your pain may not be at the surface. If that is the case for you, sit with the feeling of numbness or repression; the sensation of not feeling becomes your starting point. Simply allow whatever feeling, however trivial, to arise. You don't need to go in search of particular emotions or events. Those back rooms in your mind will unlock themselves when you are ready.

LISTENING TO YOUR INNER CHILD

I had meditated for years until my fear of the supernatural broke through and flooded my consciousness. No quick fixes are to be found here. You may want instant gratification; you're hoping your pain will just melt away. You're not alone in that desire. Most of us want to move through our pain quickly, but that's part of the avoidance of our discomfort. While sometimes our emotional pain resolves quickly—and it's a tremendously uplifting experience when it does—more often than not, your pain asks to be seen once, twice, or several times.

As you practice feeling your emotions, you will learn that sometimes, feeling an emotion is not enough. Instead, your emotions need to speak to you. They might have messages for you. They might have information, not just in the language of sensation, but in words. For when you are feeling emotional pain, you are connecting with a sliver of a former self that was wounded in some way. Your younger self came to understand some event, a clash with someone or something in the world, and it created a story to make some kind of sense of the pain, primarily to avoid it in the future. These moments are small splinters or fractures of our connection with the world. To fix those fractures, we suture ourselves together with band-aids of belief and stitches made of stories. We need some kind of mental justification or explanation that validates our pain and tells us that this is the way things are.

Whenever I am disturbed or saddened or angered by something or someone, I have learned to feel that emotion deeply and then ask myself what the emotion wants to say to me. I can recall a period not that long ago where I was overwhelmed with a kind of bleakness. No matter how much I felt into it, it would not lift. The sadness covered me like a thick resin. After many weeks of this heaviness, as I sat in the garden of a local church, I finally heard a cry from deep within that asked, "Who is going to take care of me?" It was the voice of a young version of myself who had been forced to grow up and take care of himself when his parents divorced, find the money to buy his first car, and handle college applications and financial aid on his own. My younger self had matured and assumed responsibility quickly, becoming an adult very early in life. I had never listened to the part of him that still felt lost and yearned for someone else to take care of him: *Wasn't he worthy of being cared for, instead of having to do it all on his own?* That's what he needed to ask, and I had finally listened.

It is important to remember that the story your younger selves tell you in the language of emotion is valid but not necessarily true. It's valid in that it deserves to be felt and acknowledged. You give it permission to express itself. But the reasons for its expression may not stand up to scrutiny. We have to separate these mechanisms. We can feel the emotional pain while also understanding that the story generating it is not true. For example, it's not true that I have had to take care of myself; I've had a lot of support from others. But this younger version of myself felt this way and this was his story.

Here's another example. For many years, one of my greatest

triggers was a deep-seated fear that my words would cause people harm or offend them in some way. One of the ways this fear would manifest is that when I wrote an email or sent a text and didn't hear back soon after, I would reread my messages and wonder what I had done to upset the person with whom I was corresponding. Inevitably, if I prompted with some clumsy follow-up wondering if my email had gone to spam, I would get a response explaining that my would-be interlocutor was busy or had forgotten to reply. My worry was free-floating and not rooted in any verifiable evidence; my concern for offending was unfounded. Emotions tell us some truth about ourselves—namely, my belief that a lack of response meant that my words had caused offense—but they are often not true and accurate assessments of the world.

Sometimes there are no specific memories for certain reactions to life. These memories might be unconscious and deeply buried. You might not be able to identify the source of your pain or see which version of your younger self is expressing itself. When I was in grade school, one of my untraceable fears was leaving the library and being accused of stealing books. I had never stolen a book and didn't secretly want to steal books. But my fear was that I would absentmindedly put a book in my backpack, trigger the alarm, and be accused of stealing. Every time I was about to leave the library, I would check my backpack carefully, and I always felt this intense pang of fear as I passed through the security gate. My fear was about the shame of persecution and feeling defenseless. I believed no one would believe me if I protested my innocence. Even though I couldn't trace this fear to a specific moment in my past, it was still a part of me that I had to hold tenderly until eventually it felt loved enough to leave on its own.

As these episodes suggest, pausing, feeling, and listening

almost always elicit some kind of belief about the way things are or ought to be. Sometimes that belief is about me or my identity; sometimes it is about other people. A younger version of myself crafted a belief to make sense of what transpired. In my case, these beliefs took the form of a cry for love—to be taken care of or to be seen as innocent—or for God not to see me as flawed.

Through acceptance, we meet these beliefs consciously and wholeheartedly with a sense that they are not fixed. They may be deeply rooted or entwined with many other beliefs, but they ultimately can be released or reframed through this process of meeting the emotions and listening to them. As with our emotions, we don't have to push away the thought or belief. Instead, simply accepting it, along with the emotion it generates, begins the process of dismantling it. For me, I had to hold repeatedly and with great compassion—until these feelings resolved on their own—the feeling of abandonment accompanied by the thought that no one would take care of me, the sense of rejection accompanied by the thought that I had offended someone, and the fear of persecution accompanied by the thought that I would not be seen as innocent.

YOU ARE ALREADY WHOLE

With time and tenderness, even the most painful of life events can be unpacked. The curtains cloaking the back rooms of our minds will be drawn back, their windows opened to the fresh air of acceptance. It is this courage to go within, to excavate and explore our inner world, that we each must find for ourselves. It's the practice of a lifetime of letting go of the mind's trained ways of making meaning and meeting your emotions with love.

It is commonplace in New Age spiritual communities to

refer to this process as *alchemy*. Doing so harkens back to a time when we thought we could transform lead into gold through some pseudoscientific experiment. With emotional acceptance, it often feels like some kind of pseudoscientific magic is at work. You believe that your emotion is like a rude houseguest who will move in permanently when what they really want is to stop by for a quick chat. If you listen, they'll leave. As the Buddhists say, when your demons show up, offer them tea and cake. If you pay attention, you might even figure out why they stopped by in the first place.

The purported magic here is nothing esoteric. We are transforming pain with love. The power of being accepted, just as we are, is something we have all felt; at least, I hope so. For some of us, it might be a grandparent, an aunt or uncle, or a dear friend—a person whose love we have never doubted. For me, it was my great-grandmother, a woman whose love for me was so pure that to this day, when I think of her, I feel held. When we hold our former wounded selves in the same way as these people have held us, we practice unconditional love for ourselves. That is why we can't wish our emotions away. What those parts of us seek is full and complete acceptance. They want to be loved. Not feeling loved in some way was the source of their creation. At earlier stages in our life, we experienced emotional pain and no longer felt loved. Now, those wounded parts of us want to express themselves and be held, fully and completely, through that emotion.

When you practice accepting your emotions just as they are, you expand your heart's capacity to love. You expand your capacity to be present, with compassion, to yourself. What is "the divine" but the capacity to love unconditionally, without any judgment? In this way, each time you meet your emotions with wholehearted acceptance, you strengthen your own connection with the divine inside.

Most importantly, your capacity to be loving and compassionate is not, and never was, broken or lost. It was only buried beneath the pain. Each time you peel back a layer of pain, your divine heart expands a bit more.

For some, the idea of acceptance triggers a loss of hope, as if you might be saying to yourself that you will never change and never be different. But acceptance is neither resignation nor acquiescence. The reason you lose hope is because beneath so much of our pain, at the root of it all, is the belief that we are not lovable. We reiterate our unlovability by pushing aside the parts of ourselves that cry out because they don't feel loved, and in doing so, confirm for them that they were right. Interwoven with our pain is a desire to be a different, "better" person. You cling to a future version of yourself that will be deserving of love, and so the idea of accepting yourself seems like you're acquiescing to this idea that you'll never be whole or good enough to be loved.

Accepting yourself is not throwing in the towel. This is where you meet your resistance and realize that your resistance is a form of judgment. You judge your pain when you resist it. You tell yourself that you shouldn't feel these emotions, and that there's something wrong or flawed with you for having them. Resistance is our judgment masquerading as a defense mechanism. We push our feelings aside to protect ourselves, but in truth, we're telling parts of ourselves that they are not worthy of our attention. If we refuse to hold them tenderly, we're confirming for these wounded parts that they are indeed not lovable.

ESCAPING LINEARITY

As we continue down this path, step by step, we can sometimes fall prey to an old habit of linearity and growth. When you look back, you might see a linear sense of progression. You might feel that you are better, healthier, or improved. You may feel a sense of relief or accomplishment. You might even believe that, if you continue with enough dedication and devotion, this spiritual practice will make you so entirely whole that you'll never have to feel more pain. You may start to strive to always feel more positivity and less pain. But then you hit an old pattern or an old wound opens up, something you had thought healed long ago. You might judge yourself as failing or inadequate in some way because you perceive yourself to be backsliding.

In these moments, we face the temptation of spiritual bypass. We might not choose to feel our pain because we have started to cling to a state of peace or lightness. You might turn to what is now called "toxic positivity," the desire to be positive no matter the circumstances. Those who fall prey to this tendency put on a mask of happiness. They return to repression, detaching from painful moments, which happens without fully feeling the pain. Perpetually upbeat, they suppress even a hint of negative emotion as a kind of spiritual failing.

For example, one of my clients refused to see that he was quite angry that his partner had ended their relationship. As his face contorted with anger and his voice became clipped when describing what had happened, I asked him about the emotion accompanying the story. He said he felt entirely resolved even though his voice and body were telling a different story. It was more important to him to maintain the façade of balance rather than to acknowledge feeling betrayed. Even when I pointed out to him that he was displaying signs of discomfort, he dismissed them as evidence of pain. That's bypassing.

The truth is that the more that you listen to your emotions, the deeper you dive into your psyche. The greater your love and the brighter your inner light, the darker the shadows that you will illuminate within yourself. That does not mean a spiritual path embraces a nihilistic view that life is suffering. Feeling our emotions fully does not mean we seek to suffer, even if a lot of pain will emerge in the process. Suffering is what we do now, by refusing to feel our pain. On the contrary, feeling our emotions means that we are more capable of holding the more deeply wounded parts of ourselves with compassion.

If we believe that we are supposed to be fully healed in some way, there's a risk that when we hit these moments of pain, we'll embrace a more pernicious lie that is often at work already in our minds: We are beyond repair. That is the ultimate lie—the nefarious belief buried at the floor of our psychic ocean—that we are broken and will never be healed. We hold onto the hope that we'll reach a state where we never feel pain. When faced with the pain of that belief, it's no wonder that so many of us cling to the life raft of positivity.

The practice of acceptance of our emotions is a journey back to wholeness. You come to realize that you are already whole, not because you are free of all pain but because you are actually capable of meeting your pain with compassion even when you think you might be overwhelmed. Each moment that pain punctures the present is an opportunity to deepen this divine love inside. The process can seem incremental. Healing is never linear and never finished. You will see that the healing is how you relate to each of those parts of you.

This is the fundamental message: The part of us that

remains capable of love was never broken and could never be broken. For when we accept our emotions—including our disappointment when we're still feeling an old, familiar pain—we are not really healing those parts of ourselves. We're healing the part of us that believes that feeling pain is a sign of being broken or flawed. When you see those pieces of yourself and can hold them with love, those emotions seemingly dissipate. But what is really happening is that you've stopped treating them as flaws, deficiencies, or broken parts. When we accept ourselves just as we are, our wounds no longer seem like wounds but opportunities to express love. They are a chance to practice giving comfort. Our pain serves as the portal to remind us that our capacity to love ourselves is always there.

At some point, you come to realize that the very question, "When will I be healed?" is actually the moment that you splinter yourself again. That question, harboring the deep belief that you are not already whole, is what you must meet with the greatest of compassion. This is the paradox: You are not broken or in need of healing, but you must meet this feeling with wholehearted compassion, every time it surfaces, without attaching to a future without pain.

To access compassion for myself when I feel such pain, I ask: *Do I see a cracked pane of a thousand pieces where I wish the lines had never been etched, or a stained-glass window through which the light forms an image unlike any other?* When I ask the question, I realize that the cracked lines of my psyche have distracted me from seeing the full picture of myself. This is how I remember that the wholeness is not *what* I see, but *how* I gaze at myself. When you embrace with compassion the part of you that longs to be whole, to return to some state before pain etched itself in your psyche, you can move beyond the very paradigm of healing that started you on the path in the first place.

When you see yourself in this way, not as a pane of glass that lost some pristine state of wholeness, but as the unique mosaic whose lines give you features that no one else has, you no longer see your emotions as wounds. You are a stained glass illuminated from within. Your light of awareness creates an image unlike any other. From your pain emerges a unique beauty distinct from every other human being. These pieces of pain have gifted you with the opportunity to love yourself as a singular creation. When you look upon yourself with the eyes of love, through the divine heart that was never lost, all you will see is perfection, no matter what you feel in the moment.

MATERIALITY:

YOU ARE (PART OF) NATURE

I T WAS 1994, and I was in the GAP, searching for a new pair of pants. This was not a shopping spree born out of love for fast fashion. The truth is that my current wardrobe no longer fit. The antidepressant I was taking had triggered a dramatic metabolic shift, and I gained over fifty pounds in a few months' time. Once a skinny reed, I was on the verge of waddling, uncomfortable and embarrassed, as the waist size on my pants kept rising. In my early twenties, I had opted for a quick fix for an emotional issue, and my body paid the price.

I resented my body's new fat deposits and longed for my old metabolism. To my dismay, every bite was a skirmish in the battle of the bulge, and no amount of diet and exercise brought me back to my previously trim figure. I had gone from loving my body to hating it. Years later, far removed from the effects of the antidepressant, my metabolism eventually returned.

This is not, however, a tale about perseverance in the face of weight gain. It is about how we are often at war with our bodies. We beat them into submission, nip and tuck them, judge and criticize them, or attempt to ignore them. As we saw last chapter, the emotional pain that we have pushed aside ends up buried in our sinews and bones until it erupts again to be fully accepted. We turn our bodies into repositories of emotional pain. To add insult to injury, we then heap upon our bodies more pain by judging their flaws, ignoring their needs, and refusing to love them just as they are.

At first blush, spirituality might seem like a place of acceptance and love for our bodies, a space where we come to honor our bodies as precious gifts. Yoga and meditation, for example, place our awareness on our bodies and our breath. Very often, however, spiritual seekers try to move past the body, pushing aside its desires and needs. Sometimes our bodies are denigrated for containing so much craving, hunger, and lust. The Buddha famously tried to reach enlightenment through ascetic practices—fasting and depriving the body of sleep and pleasure—only to realize that it did little to release him from the ego's attachment to suffering. Despite learning this lesson eons ago, we continue to hold fast to the belief that spiritual growth is gained by denial of our materiality. Sometimes we go so far as to reject the entire material world as illusory.

Denial of our body or escaping it is not the path to connecting with the divine inside. Your body is literally time made into matter. You embody eons of evolution, genetic material passed down from one generation to the next. You are made of stardust and timeless elements. No matter how old you are, you're ancient matter repurposed. You're also a host of old ideas about the body—traditional and outdated perspectives on what's right or wrong. You're a product of humanity's effort to distinguish itself from nature.

Our bodies are not separate from nature, and nature has much more wisdom than we realize. In fact, our lives have been so divorced from nature and its consciousness that we barely understand it. We certainly do not respect, as a species, our connection to nature. We've ravaged the planet, spoiling the environment and provoking massive changes to the climate as the planet, a living ecosystem, attempts to reset the balance. We live the majority of our lives in the realm of the electronic, through images and screens, keeping nature and its wonders at bay. In so doing, we fail to grasp our interconnectedness with nature. Nature and the divine are not mutually exclusive realms. Nature is fully part of the divine. That is why our connection to the divine does not demand we transcend the body or the physical realm. We are not separate from nature, and we shouldn't try to be. We deepen our connection with the divine inside not when we escape our body and nature, but when we fully embrace them both.

LOVING YOUR BODY

How many of us can say that we love our bodies fully and completely? Most of us cannot. We are confronted with messages about our bodies from a very early age. We're told not to pick our noses or touch certain parts of ourselves. We learn very quickly that nudity is problematic. We're bombarded constantly with messages about which bodies are attractive and which ones are not. Cultural and religious messages about sexuality and desire permeate our understanding of what's right and wrong. In addition to having all sorts of beliefs about our bodies, we do all sorts of things to our bodies, like feeding them suboptimal foods and plying them with all manner of substances. We then judge our bodies, finding certain parts attractive but quibbling with others. We might even "love" our bodies but shape and sculpt them to satisfy exacting standards of beauty. So rarely do we practice accepting them just as they are.

It's odd that we make this precious container of life into a repository for shame. Nowhere is our aversion to our bodies—and our rejection of nature—more apparent than our ways of treating the very act that gave rise to our lives: sex. Despite sex's centrality to our existence, spirituality and religion have a terrible track record when it comes to reproducing puritanical and misguided norms about sexuality.

The spiritual tendency is to repress our sexuality. Yet the effort to suppress our body's most natural urges inevitably leads to their emergence through abuse or scandal. As Freud taught us long ago, the repressed always returns. No tradition seems immune. Catholic priests have abused young parishioners for decades, with little accountability imposed by the institution. In the yoga world, Bikram Choudhury, who fashioned a brand of hot yoga, was exposed for multiple sexual abuses and fled to Mexico. After Sri K. Pattabhi Jois, the founder of Ashtanga yoga, died in 2009, many victims came forth to share their stories of abuse. Similarly, the spiritual leader of Kripalu, Amrit Desai, scandalized his community and fled when it was discovered he was sleeping with a student.

The history of Buddhism in the United States fares little better. Three of the four Zen masters who arrived in the 1960s were later found to have engaged in serious sexual misconduct; the fourth was succeeded by his student, who soon enveloped the San Francisco Zen Center in its own sex scandal. In the Tibetan tradition known as Shambhala, Ösel Tendzin, the successor to Chögyam Trungpa Rinpoche, contracted HIV and had unprotected sex with several students, whom he did not forewarn of the risk. In 2019, an investigation confirmed that Sakyong Mipham Rinpoche, the current head, had abused female members of the sangha.

Sexual shadows in spiritual lineages often emerge, with traumatic consequences to students, because the hierarchical structure rooted in a singular (male) authority figure often enables such misdeeds to go unchecked. Worse still, the teacher may attempt to justify the abuse as part of the student's spiritual growth—a form of spiritual gaslighting. But the problem isn't just having a guru at the top of the pyramid. Spirituality has a sexual problem because it continues to be hampered by antiquated views of sexuality as sin or "dangerous" energy.

There's nothing inherently wrong about sexual energy or desire. It's a natural part of being human. It's part of our capacity to create and our desire to connect. Yet we treat it with such disdain, heap stigma upon it, and above all, attempt to repress it. How many of us can enjoy a sexual, consensual relationship with full abandon to our desire? Without any shroud or hint of judgment? How many of us can be honest about our desires without questioning whether they are right?

We cloak our desires with a veil of social opprobrium rather than treating them as the natural impulses they are. As a result, we are not taught to be deeply aware of our sexual desires, how to be with them, or how to work with the stories we tell ourselves when they emerge. Like all human relationships, issues of power, consent, and free will come into play. No doubt sex can be used to harm, but most of the harm ensues from treating sex as a dangerous activity that must be shrouded in shame and secrecy.

So much of what we do is to deprive ourselves of pleasure rather than fully allow ourselves to experience it. Spiritual seekers often treat sex as a kind of lowly activity, reflecting base desires that are antithetical to the divine. Between consenting adults, though, sex can be a divine act, allowing two people to share these unique forms and enjoy a pleasure that our bodies were designed to experience. It is one path for connecting to the energy of life within you. In that way, sexual energy is divine—it is the energy that seeks to create. This is not to deny that sex can invite all sorts of issues, because having sex has consequences, whether that's as simple as bringing up emotions, navigating different expectations about what sex means for each person, contracting diseases, pregnancy, and more. Sex is not simple. But it is not, in and of itself, morally tainted. Sex should be enjoyed without judgment, without any sense that it might be a violation of some spiritual law.

* * *

Outside of the realm of sex, how often do you appreciate your body? Do you see it as a divine temple needing to be cared for and loved? Do you praise it or belittle it? If we were able to love our bodies completely, to be in full acceptance of our physical forms, our consciousness would undergo a dramatic shift. Most of us take on a lot of shame around our physical forms. Society reinforces this by reminding us on a daily basis through advertising that a very limited range of bodies are considered attractive, so much so that we applaud as revolutionary any ad campaign that represents normal bodies with all of their lumpy grandeur.

Can you stand in front of a mirror and stare at your body lovingly? Do so and notice how much you want to turn away, or how often your eyes gravitate to the parts of you that you'd like to be different. Having gone through wild shifts in weight over the course of my lifetime, I can point to fat deposits and protrusions that I would prefer were flatter. There's no point in pretending that I haven't carried shame in my body.

During a retreat in the Amazon working with ayahuasca, I released an enormous amount of shame from my body. The plant medicine pointed me to parts of my body that I had wanted to change and explained why they were the way they were. With this purging, I was able to stand naked, without fear of judgment. This is just one of countless episodes where I have learned that we ignore our divinity when we make our body the villain of our spiritual lives. It is by loving our physicality, fully and completely, that we experience spiritual transcendence by releasing that judgmental part of our consciousness.

Sex and nudity are not the only ways that we regard our relationship to bodily pleasure with suspicion or derision. The mundane pleasures of eating and drinking are also laden with shame. For those on a spiritual path, a kind of vigilance some-times takes root. We feel a need to eat in certain ways—organic, vegetarian or vegan, raw, nothing processed, no sugar, no alco-hol—and along the way, a certain amount of judgment enters. Abstinence or refraining from eating with child-like abandon are ways of depriving ourselves of an experience that we should enjoy wholeheartedly.

That is not a call for us to abandon awareness of what is best for our bodies, nor for us to embrace hedonism. Excessive pleasure has its consequences. I've eaten things that I craved only to discover that my body really didn't want that much sugar. But all too often we develop an unhealthy vigilance, eval-uating each and every bite we might take for its potential effect on our spiritual journey.

I recall a time when my intuition led me on a journey through the streets of Manhattan to a bakery I had never encountered. There I discovered one of the most delicious cookies I had ever had. I could have rejected that entire epi-sode based on some very narrow views about what is and isn't right for a spiritual diet. I relished it, allowing my taste buds to savor that concoction of butter and chocolate. Eating can be a truly spiritual act when you enjoy the sensual delights it offers. It is natural to feel pleasure. Our bodies are designed for it. To do so, we must slow down and eat our food with exquisite attention to the experience. This is one way that we honor the body as nature.

We also honor our material being when we do not deprive ourselves of what our bodies truly need. On that same ayahuasca retreat, the plant medicine told me I was much too hard on my body when it came to eating meat. For years, I had been taught that I had to be a vegetarian or vegan to be spiritual. Hearing this message about eating animal flesh made me sob. I knew already that at the end of the retreat there would be a large meal at which chicken would be served. The ayahuasca said to me pointedly, "I want you to eat the chicken." I cried out that I didn't want the chickens to suffer. She explained that they don't suffer; they understand the cycle of life, and my body would need the chicken's strength when our work together was done.

Heeding the ayahuasca's request, I went to the chicken coop the day before the final retreat meal. A lone white chicken, among several gray ones, stepped forward as I crouched in front of the chicken wire. She leaned her beak against the cage so that I could touch her. I stared into her eyes, and she didn't move away. At that moment I knew that she was the chicken I would eat, and somehow it felt like she knew it too. I had never before communed with a chicken in this way, locking eyes and allowing for a soulful connection. I thanked her for her sacrifice, and she stepped away.

The cook confirmed the next day at lunch that the white chicken had been slaughtered that morning for our meal. I obeyed the ayahuasca's request and ate that chicken with a reverence I had never before felt. Having been stripped so bare for three days, my body needed that sustenance for the long trip home. Her death gave me life, and my body was thankful for that gift. Since then, I have learned to honor my body's needs, eating meat on occasion as my body requests it. Nature itself taught me to let go of self-judgment and accept that at times my body needs to eat meat.

The shame and deprivation we impose on our physical being around the pleasure of food show up in our enormous collective discomfort around the process of digestion. The by-products of eating, the most basic and life-giving task our bodies require of us, are feces and flatulence. Yet we attach to them so much shame.

At the same meditation retreat where my childhood fears of the supernatural were released, I found myself straining for a different kind of release: Eating high-fiber meals while remaining fairly sedentary had made me quite gassy. I'm sure I wasn't alone. Yet, despite sitting on the meditation cushion in a room full of a hundred strangers, I had not myself passed gas, nor had I heard any kind of fart erupting into the hallowed meditation hall. The irony is that I had been hearing quite clearly the near-constant gurgling of people's digestive systems. The hall was actually quite active with a cacophony of churning and twisting, popping and squishing, punctuated with an occasional burp or cough. Amid all of that digestive din, the sound of passing gas was remarkably absent. The only conclusion I could draw was that either everyone else at the retreat had access to some world-renowned probiotic, or there were a lot of clenched sphincters in the room.

By turns perplexed and piqued, I realized that in all of my years meditating, I had never heard anyone pass gas in a meditation hall or heard any teacher comment on flatulence during meditation. Despite being a normal part of human life, was the humble fart a too minor or too uncomfortable topic of teaching? Flatulence inspires all kinds of aversion in individuals— aversion to unpleasant odors, aversion to shame, aversion to acknowledging our biological reality. That opprobrium extends to even talking about farting, especially in the rarefied space of a meditation retreat.

After one of the retreat teachers reminded us to "allow the mind to open to the full range of human experience," I wondered why that didn't seem to include passing gas. During the day's Q&A period, I asked: "How do we practice with passing gas in the meditation hall?" The meditation hall erupted in laughter, and the teacher, not the slightest bit unnerved, acknowledged the room's collective response: "I guess you heard the question!" The teacher responded that the practice was the same as with any other phenomena—to work with the aversion to passing gas, to the smell and sound, and if the gas were excessive, to kindly spare one's fellow meditators by leaving the hall.

In allowing ourselves to pass gas, we allow our natural selves to emerge and be experienced in their fullness. The same is true of defecation. We treat the waste products of our body as if they were sinful rather than the natural process of life and death that they are. We return a part of our body to the earth when we defecate. That which no longer serves us returns to the ground, where it can in turn create new life to sustain other living beings.

These processes of the body—sex, eating, and digestion—remind us that we are indelibly connected with nature, not separate from it. Our aversion is a reflection of how we denigrate our relationship to nature.

THE CONSCIOUSNESS OF NATURE

Although we profoundly misunderstand nature and routinely disavow our connection to it, we are also often drawn to it, filled with fascination at its marvels or comforted by it. Many of us spend time in nature because we find it peaceful, invigorating, or consoling. Gardening, hiking, camping, spending time at the beach—these are all forms of connecting with the natural world.

When I sit in nature, a familiar feeling of tranquility washes over me. No doubt many of you feel something similar. At first blush, you might think that nature provides us this relief because we enjoy a respite from the chaos and frenetic energy of electronic life, social media, and interpersonal conflict. It's true that nature allows us to escape the humdrum of work or the frantic pace of modern life. But nature is not always peaceful. Trees can sway perilously in the wind. Rain can hammer the earth. Indulge in a few nature documentaries, and you'll remember that nature is often a violent spectacle of feast and famine. Ask mountain climbers, surfers, and other intrepid explorers of the world, and you'll hear plenty of stories about how nature can be punishing.

What nature offers is something more than a tranquil escape from the demands of adult life. When we find ourselves at rest in a forest, at the beach, in the mountains, by a lake, or sitting in a garden, we connect with a different form of consciousness. Indigenous cultures have long understood that nature has a consciousness that we simply cannot access from our conventional minds and typical senses.[1] It is a consciousness that Western science is only now beginning to recognize. When we surround ourselves in nature, we return to our inherent connection with the material world that we have forgotten by insulating ourselves and by denigrating our bodies. What distinguishes human consciousness from nature is our incessant pursuit of self. Even when they are quaking, lashing out, or swirling madly, the earth, the wind, and the rain do not ask themselves who they are and why they are here.

It is not the respite from modern life that nature truly offers, but relief from an existential question that plagues us as human beings. By seeing ourselves as separate from nature, we overlook that nature is itself, without asking if it should be some other way, and without questioning whether other parts of nature should change, if they're good enough, or if they have purpose. Each part of nature serves to allow the other parts of nature to exist in dynamic equilibrium. We too can be this way, if we are willing to simply be in our bodies just as they are.

Rekindling our connection to the natural world begins by slowing down and allowing our bodies to touch the earth. We reclaim our status as part of nature when we recognize that we breathe air, drink water, eat plants that have grown from the earth's soil and animals that have eaten those plants, and soak up sunlight. We owe our lives to photosynthesis. Remember that you are the sun, the wind, the water, and the earth. This is not a poetic claim to truth; it is physics.[2] Each moment you take the natural world into you and release some of yourself back to it. Reminding yourself that you are nature can allow you to feel more ease in your skin when shame and lack of self-love reassert themselves.

When we reclaim our connection to nature, we might find ourselves gravitating to certain elements more than others. Perhaps you are drawn to water, to its depth and connection to emotion, or to its capacity to flow, to move with ease, and to transform into both solid and vapor. Or you might be drawn to the heat and transformative power of fire, with its capacity to reduce to the building blocks of nature and become part of the earth again. You might be drawn to the wind, with its constant movement, yet connected with everything. Perhaps you find attractive the earth itself, with the fortitude of stone and dirt to anchor and hold you. These elements can tell us something about ourselves and our nature.

I was on a retreat at Omega, a spiritual center in upstate New York, when I began to feel the pull of the rock. I was not usually drawn to rock, its density and sense of being anchored; more often I have been drawn to water and air. Sitting on a stone, feeling its hardness, its capacity to remain in one place, its capacity to weather harsh conditions, to be slowly eroded by wind and air yet resilient in the face of change, I could see how developing those qualities would be beneficial. I was often too quick to embrace change and move on, to flow without any resistance, thus embodying air and water. The immovability of stone, however, felt foreign to me, even though healthy boundaries are essentially the element of stone being brought to bear on human relationships.[3]

At times, specific aspects of nature have offered their wisdom. A holly tree outside my bedroom window has served as a guide and a reminder of the power of trees to be both rooted and flexible, to endure with the thick skin of their bark, to offer support with their branches, to allow parts of themselves to be stripped away so that new growth might happen. Their capacity to weather wind, rain, and snow, to adapt and grow in ways that make do with the soil they are given, their capacity to reach up to the light and down into the earth at the same time—these are qualities I have had to cultivate in myself. Finding the ways that nature speaks to us, whether through plants, animals, or elements, is part of reclaiming our relationship to nature.

Among the many marvels I have experienced is the way that the earth itself is a direct conduit for powerful spiritual energy. On a flat rock in Sedona, for example, I sat quietly and began to feel strength and confidence rise up from my seat and throughout my limbs. The longer I sat, the stronger this sensation grew.

I was sitting on what is known as a vortex. It might sound ludicrous to skeptical ears, but that particular spot filled me with conviction and a desire for action. Other vortexes in Sedona give off different energies—some are heart-opening and softening, while others provide a sense of balance and equilibrium.

It was not the first time that a particular geographic spot had altered me in an energetic way. Every time I visit the island of Kauai, something almost miraculous happens. Within just a few days, I start to feel emotionally raw, as if I have been working through some kind of deep emotional issue and layers of mental self-protection have been pulled away, leaving me tender and vulnerable, almost prickly. By contrast with the willful zeal imparted by Sedona, Kauai leaves me with a sense that some kind of scab has been lifted, baring fresh, tender skin. It's not always immediately clear what has been lifted from me, but the island gently burnishes some part of me so that a new aspect of myself can emerge.

ANIMAL CONSCIOUSNESS

The elements and the earth are not the only parts of nature that offer us guidance and remind us how little we understand of nature. Nowhere else is nature more mysterious than in our understanding of animal consciousness. The phrase itself might raise some hackles, as it is a longstanding debate among ethologists whether animals have consciousness or cognition. Throughout human history, we have placed ourselves at the top of the pyramid, reflecting a deep-seated insecurity and need to reassure ourselves that we are somehow the best. That is no longer the prevailing view among scientists, who now, as summarized so artfully by Frans de Waal, rightly refer to human cognition as just one type of animal cognition.[4] In his work, he points out that we used to project our understanding of what counts as cognition on animals without recognizing the unique nature of each species and how their needs and skills are best understood.

A similar message was given to me during an ayahuasca ceremony in which I found myself losing the capacity to speak. Unable to produce more than guttural noises, I thought to myself, *I feel like an animal,* and the plant medicine replied forcefully, "You do not understand animals. None of you does." Indeed, de Waal provides numerous examples of how we, as humans, have underestimated other species because we projected ourselves onto them. Scientists have often assumed that animals were less cognitively developed than humans and could not perform tasks that come easily to us. Nevertheless, when experimenters have attempted to look at the world from the animal's perspective, they have had to ask themselves a different question: What motivates this animal's actions in the world? By asking that question instead, de Waal explains, scientists have been able to recognize that animals can use tools, cooperate, and show empathy.[5] Animals also demonstrate the ability to remember and plan for the future, revealing that they have a relationship to time we usually only associate with humans.[6] In that way, animal consciousness is often far more refined than we have previously assumed.

Take, for example, the wisdom of bees. Jacqueline Freeman, an expert beekeeper, has written about the consciousness of bees and how it differs from human consciousness.[7] Bees embody unity, with each bee's singularity subordinated to the wholeness of the hive; that kind of connection is anathema to our human minds. Each bee in a hive, Freeman explains, experiences what every other bee experiences. We are not bees; as humans we are very much limited by our individual selves, and our preoccupation with the safety and security of our bodies.

We have much to learn from animals. Our efforts to understand them reveal to us our blind spots, assumptions, and habits of thought that are deeply limiting. Letting go of our penchant for assuming that consciousness only takes certain forms is part of us relinquishing our effort to distinguish ourselves from nature and ask instead what we have in common. As it stands, we know that at the level of DNA, we share far more than we differ.[8]

Personally, no animal has taught me as much about animal consciousness as cats. Pop culture and social media often portray cats as a kind of Zen master, as if they were always in the present moment. But my cats, Charlie and Lily, experience all sorts of mood swings and emotions. They have their preferences about being rubbed, which toys they like, and their food. They are also inscrutable. They might suddenly go berserk, staring wildly at some unseen spirit or hunting an invisible prey. I do not understand them, yet I can see that we are all part of nature. We eat, sleep, and poop. We rest and play. We have cravings for treats. I revel in our communion yet honor the fact that I will never fully understand them.

In the end, the main difference between them and us is that they don't judge themselves. As far as I know, Lily doesn't look at her fur and compare its texture to Charlie's. She doesn't stare at the mirror and wonder if she should straighten her teeth or if her coat should be thicker. What my journey with nature has taught me is that the human mind, which we think makes us superior to nature, gives us the capacity to feel bad about ourselves in ways that nature, in all of its varieties of consciousness, does not. The trees, the birds, and the bees don't ask if they're pretty or lovable. The flower bud doesn't ask if it needs to bloom just right to be accepted. Nature offers a valuable lesson about being true to ourselves without existential angst. Nature asks us to accept ourselves as material beings who are part of a world that we will never fully understand. It is, paradoxically, when we accept our materiality that we find a certain kind of transcendence from the limitations of human life.

CLIMATE CHANGE

Nature expands our understanding of consciousness, pushing ourselves out of our definitions so that we are just one example of nature's possibility. In embracing our status as nature, we can come to a place of humility and wonder in the face of so much diversity and difference. We can also appreciate that nature operates as a complex yet delicate ecosystem, one that we do not fully understand. Nature demands a certain kind of equilibrium. The same is true of our bodies if they are given the right balance of nutrition, rest, and exercise. When we are out of balance, illness sets in.

Nowhere is our lack of balance and our confusion about our relationship to nature more apparent than climate change. The heating of the planet is evidence of our fundamental misunderstanding of nature. Humanity is now the cause of planetary illness. Our pollution has had devastating effects on the weather; our mistreatment of the bees and soil is having pernicious effects on our food system. We rip fossil fuels from the earth to burn for fuel and then expel enormous amounts of carbon monoxide and methane that cause the planet to heat up. The melting of the polar ice caps, the rising sea levels, the acidification and pollution of the oceans cannot be ignored.

We are quickly moving to a state where the planet will not

be able to sustain human life. That is a remarkable statement. We are using our powers of creation to create a world in which we will have no place. We refuse to address the ways that we are out of balance with nature. We know what needs to be done, but we seem incapable of doing it.

We talk now of engineering the weather rather than eliminating fossil fuels and devoting our resources to renewable forms of energy. Radical proposals like attempting to cool the planet through geoengineering are now on the table. Such ideas were once the purview of science fiction movies, but now they grace the pages of science journals and United Nations reports. Human beings have barely understood the weather enough to predict it with reasonable certainty a few days in advance, yet we think we know enough to alter an immensely complex ecosystem through artificial means.

This is hubris, born from our ignorance of nature's complexity. We are hastening our collective demise because we do not want to deal with the changes that truly healing climate change would impose on us. But our hubris also stems from the fact that we have not yet learned that we, too, are nature. We need to embrace what that means. We need to understand ourselves as integral parts of a vast ecosystem in which humans are but one actor. Some might liken our turn to geoengineering to taking an antidepressant, a necessary but temporary step, only to discover that there may be side effects and consequences that we never anticipated. Unfortunately, the likely effects are going to be much more devastating than having to buy a pair of husky jeans at the GAP.

The fundamental lesson that nature teaches us is that our current consciousness is proving to be our downfall. We act as if we were superior when, in truth, we are profoundly ignorant. Just as we cannot ignore or transcend our bodies, we cannot ignore the planet. We have no other to inhabit. Instead, it is with humility and affection for our physicality that we should meet this challenge. Just as we must love and take care of our bodies, so too must we take care of the planet. That is the way that we honor the divine spirit that runs through all of creation. Nature, in the guise of climate change, is telling humanity that the time for us to learn this critical lesson is quickly running out.

AWARENESS:
YOU ARE ALWAYS AND NEVER
IN THE PRESENT

IMAGINE, FOR A moment, that you could not recall any memories, nor the emotions that accompany them. Your personal history would be erased. You would remember neither your immediate family nor the prior generations that led to you. Your body would seem like a mystery to you, and you would have no memories tied to its growth and change. You would quickly realize that you had fallen out of step with time.

In Christopher Nolan's 2000 film, *Memento*, something similar happens to the main character, Leonard, who suffers from retrograde amnesia. He cannot form new memories, and every fifteen minutes or so, he reverts to the last state he could remember. As a result, he concocts an elaborate system of Polaroids, tattoos, and notes to himself to keep track of the people he knows and has met, what role they've played in his life, and most of all, whether he can trust them. He is in pursuit of his wife's murderer, and Leonard knows that many of the people around him are not trustworthy and take advantage of his amnesia (like the hotel clerk who rents him two rooms).

Unable to form new memories, Leonard is out of step with time. As he says quite poignantly, "How do I heal, if I can't feel time?" It turns out, though, that Leonard is also not trustworthy:

Knowing that he will forget the next fifteen minutes, he selectively chooses what messages to leave himself, thus crafting the narrative that he will recreate the next time his memory resets. Leonard chooses to create his perception of the present by selectively manipulating the little that he remembers.

In many ways, the film offers something of a nightmare scenario in which we live in a world where everything is unfamiliar and untrustworthy. It is the kind of nightmare that anybody who suffers from memory loss can understand. In so doing, it reminds us of the centrality of time in our lives, for we rely on our capacity to navigate time to perform the most basic tasks as human beings. It is also a parable about how we selectively take in time, form memories, and craft our view of the world. We are all, in some way, just like Leonard.

Time is the crucible for our lives. To be clear, when we speak of time, we are talking about at least two different concepts. On the one hand, we must grapple with clock time. We have a birth date, our entry point into this world, and we have an unknown end point, the date and time of our death. Between those two poles, time flows inexorably forward. We contend with this flow of time by scheduling, planning, and coordinating our lives. We are governed by our shared commitment to clocks and calendars. We have to book appointments and make plans with others. We set aside vast amounts of time for eating and sleeping. Our lives are constant negotiations with the sands of the hourglass.

Yet even as time's arrow flows forward, our minds constantly navigate psychological time. This is our individual perception of time, whether our minds are on the past, present, or future, as well as how we measure the passage of clock time. We get bored and talk of "wasting time" or "killing time," so we want time to speed up. When we get immersed in activities and our minds stop paying as much attention to clock time, we remark that "time flies" and might even want time to slow down a bit. Our lives are filled with conflicts with clock time: We worry that we don't have enough time to complete tasks, or we'll be late for some appointment. The present moment is somehow pinched between these impulses from the past and the pressures of the future. We are immersed in psychological time even as we advance through clock time.

Despite time's centrality in our lives, explanations for what time is or how it works elude us. As the theoretical physicist Carlo Rovelli writes, "The nature of time is perhaps the greatest remaining mystery."[1] As Rovelli explains, one school of thought, from Aristotle, has treated time as the measure of change; if we do not perceive any change, time has not passed. Another school of thought, from Newton, has argued that time is itself independent from us so that even if there was no change, time still passes. According to Rovelli, Einstein reconciled these views by showing that time and space exist, but that they are not independent of us. We are literally time and space, each of us. We are inseparable from the fabric of spacetime. If that seemed the end of the debate, it nevertheless simply shifted grounds so that physicists now debate the consequences for our theories of time at the quantum level, where it seems time ceases to exist in the smallest dimensions of our reality.[2]

Time remains a mystery for physicists and spiritualists alike. The riddle of time infuses the questions that we ask ourselves as human beings. When we grapple with existential questions like whether we are timeless souls who will depart this plane for another realm, or if our consciousness is finite and comes to an end with death, we are grappling with how our perception of time makes us feel. What ultimately matters to those on a spiritual path is how we feel about time and the meaning it has for our understanding of life.

It is not surprising, then, that being in the present moment, or the now, as a form of liberation from our existential angst, has become a touchstone. The phrase "be here now" was made famous by Ram Dass with his eponymously titled work of spiritual wisdom. The concept has been a part of contemporary spirituality ever since then and arguably reached its zenith with Eckhart Tolle's *The Power of Now*. Hence, by contrast with the painful amnesia experienced by Leonard in *Memento*, in which he lives in a constant present that he cannot remember, spiritual wisdom proclaims that we become whole again when we repair our relationship to time by letting go of the past and the future. If we are in the present moment, we are told, we will discover peace and contentment. Is the path of liberation really about releasing ourselves from the past and the future? Is transcendence about *escaping* time?

BEING PRESENT TO THE PRESENT

To understand the role of time in spirituality, we must first understand two key concepts: what it means to be present and what it means to be in the present moment. These are not the same.

Most of the time, we are not present to our lives. For example, when we face a major challenge or upheaval, we very often review what led up to the event in an effort to understand what went wrong. We retrace our steps, going back over the steps leading up to whatever it is we are facing, and sometimes regret fills us. We often conclude that we made a choice that we now wish we had not made. We chose one path and now we wish we had picked something else. You are discontent with your life in some way, and now you rewind in your mind the steps you have chosen so that you might have ended up elsewhere. Perhaps you are unhappy with your current job or profession, and you go back in time to the moment you made your decision and fantasize about going in a different direction. Perhaps you're just stuck in traffic, and you think that you should not have hit the snooze button more than once.

Whatever the situation, you are in one place, and you now imagine that you would be in a better one if you could go back in time and make a different choice. Of course, it is equally plausible that if you had made that different choice in the first place, you might still be unhappy. You can imagine that the alternative version of yourself, the one who made the choice you wish you had, is sitting somewhere else, imagining they would have been happier making the choice you did. That's the riddle of regret. We often think the other choice would have led to a happier outcome, which we can never know for certain. In other words, you are resisting what is happening now and refuse to remain present to it, preferring instead to imagine you could be elsewhere if only you had made different choices.

Part of the spiritual path is accepting that we cannot escape time. We are memory and history made flesh. Our memories are repositories of information in the form of emotions that thrust themselves into the present moment. Our bodies are these wondrous repositories of historical memory and genetic material, carrying the traces of generations past. I cannot alter the facts that I was born on a particular date, that I inherited DNA from my parents, or that my body bears stretch marks from the year I took an antidepressant in my twenties. Indeed, our most recent scientific understanding tells us, contrary to the fantasies of science fiction films like *The Terminator* or *Hot*

Tub Time Machine, that the past is past and cannot be altered.[3] We need not worry that pesky robots could come back and kill the mother of humanity's future savior or that four unsuccessful high school friends might travel through a hot tub to the past and use their knowledge of the stock market to produce a new, fabulously rich future.

On a psychological level, the past also seems fixed. Our memories, emotions, and body all measure and record both clock and psychological time for us. Hence, the promise of mindfulness is that if you place your attention on the present moment and avoid thinking about other moments of time, you can experience a sense of peace. If you spend any amount of time inspecting your past or envisioning the future, you begin to realize how much you are trapped between the pain of the past and anxiety about the future. Between those two dimensions of time, the present beckons as a respite for the agitated mind. If you can stop ruminating on what has already transpired and cannot be changed, if you can stop worrying about what has yet to transpire and cannot be controlled, you can find peace by being here now.

But time and the mind are more complicated than this presentation of mindfulness might suggest. The power of the present moment is not found in *ignoring* certain dimensions of time. When we treat the present moment as the goal of our awareness, in an effort to keep our attention in one temporal dimension and away from the other two, we miss an important insight. Being focused on the present moment does not deny your relationship to time, as if you had no past and no future. That's because when you think about the past or the future, you do so only in the present moment.[4] In fact, that's the only moment in which you can think about the past and the future, because that is the only moment in which your mind performs its mental activity.

The difference between the past, the present, and the future is simply the data that your mind contemplates. If you're focused on the present, your mind is paying attention to the data you are receiving through your senses—principally, sight, touch, and hearing—right now. That focus might also include the thoughts and images you form in your mind in response to that sensory data. If you're focused on the past, your mind is placing its attention on mental images that you create based on prior experiences. The past is a construct of the mind that you access in the present moment by conjuring up memories. When you remember, your mind reconstructs a prior moment in the present. The same is true of the future. You are imagining, anticipating, fantasizing, and creating possibilities of what might be based on data that already exists in your mind. You are here now, imagining what might transpire, and that imagining is often coupled with emotional reactions. Whether you're thinking about what you'll have for lunch or what you might watch on Netflix this evening, or planning a trip, or making plans to meet a dear friend, your mental activity is taking place in the present.

A distinction now arises between being in the present—which we always are—and being present. You can be very present to what is occurring in you or around you, which is the path of acceptance. You can also deeply resist it, push it away, try to cram it back into your mental attic in the hopes of not having to deal with it. Your level of acceptance or resistance to your mental activity (and emotional reactions) determines how present you are. It's not enough to simply keep your attention on the present; the question is whether you're in a state of resistance or acceptance to what is arising in the present.

This confusion between being in the present and being present routinely plays out in a certain version of spiritual wisdom that denigrates the past and the future as the source of suffering. It is not thinking about the past or the future that creates suffering, but your emotional response to your thinking that creates suffering. Most often, our minds are focused on some event in the past or possibility in the future because of the emotions they generate. Very often, we are pulled to the past because we have unresolved emotional pain, and we are pulled to the future because we feel fear and insecurity about our lives.

But we experience those emotions now, in the present moment. We can just as easily recoil from the emotions generated by what is happening right in front of us and attempt to distract ourselves. This is what happens when you're bored at work or fighting with a family member—you don't want to be present to those feelings, which are happening currently, and you look to flee or get away rather than face them. All of that mental activity takes place in the present, but being present to it—that is, remaining with it and not searching for some other kind of mental activity—is the truly hard part.

This distinction between being present and being in the present moment means that even when we proclaim to be in the present moment, we are often not focused on what is right in front of us. We may be focused instead on something else in our lives, some emotionally charged event that may even be happening contemporaneously, but that is not directly clamoring for our attention in that very moment. This is what happens when you sit with a friend in a coffee shop and spend your time complaining about your job or your spouse; the job or that other person is not right in front of you at that moment, your friend is. You've dragged the past—say, a prior conflict at work with your boss or an argument with your spouse from this morning—into this present moment with your friend. You are no longer present to your friend, to the coffee, to what is transpiring around you, or to what your friend is sharing because your mind is still thinking about that argument with your spouse.

In fact, part of the reason that we drift to the past or the future is because we do not want to *be present to the present moment*. Our minds resist what is happening. That is why when we are actually focused on the present moment, it does not automatically translate to peace, happiness, and joy. You can just as easily be in the present moment in a state of anger, resistance, or fear, as you can be with it in a state of peace. You can be really, dreadfully bored with it, as any meditator who has sat for a long retreat can tell you. You can berate the present moment and not be happy about it. Again, you can have an emotional reaction to what is happening right before your eyes.

New meditators quickly discover how hard it is to be present. It's one of the reasons that meditation and mindfulness, while reaching a mainstream popularity, are also the subject of many criticisms. Mindfulness and meditation are not the cure-alls that modern, Western interpretations of spirituality purport them to be. Many people meditate and claim that it does nothing for them, that it is impossible to sit still and be with their thoughts. You may think you're in the now when you're simply becoming aware of all the thoughts passing through your mind in the present moment. You're not in the now if you do not want to remain present to that activity. The present moment, rather than offering respite, becomes a source of distress. In the face of so much frenzied mental activity happening in real time, the peace offered by the present moment seems to elude us.

* * *

The purpose of meditation is not to deny your awareness of the past or the future, but rather to strengthen and stabilize your mind's ability to remain with whatever comes into its awareness. That is what it means to remain present. Although you might be overwhelmed when you become present to the frenetic activity of your mind, when you slowly deepen your awareness of this mental activity, you can begin to watch it from a distance. You might begin to bring some compassionate awareness to your mental activity, simply noting where your mind goes. The point is not to stop the thoughts or deal with the emotions that accompany them. Instead, it is to watch them. You observe how your mind, always in the present moment, constantly flutters from past to future, to the present, to the past, and back again. Your mind is a time machine. It retraces your steps, viewing the world up close and from afar, teleporting you to a future world of fantasy and back to the present. When you meditate, you learn to see what your mind does with each moment. Does it take you to the past, to the future, or to what is happening around you right now?

Being present to what arises in the mind is the starting place for accepting the present moment just as it is. It is the same practice of being present to our emotions that we discussed in Chapter 1. When our memories pull up painful episodes from our past, we meet them with compassion and wisdom, knowing that they are parts of ourselves rooted in a different moment of time now revisiting us. They are our psychic ghosts. Being present does not mean avoiding them, but rather watching them from a place of love.

The more we can resolve our emotional conflicts from the past, the easier it becomes to remain present to that which arises in the present moment. If we lack the stability of mind to be present and watch what arises, we can drown in our past sorrows and become overwhelmed by our fears of what is yet to pass. The energy of the past floods us, and we lose a sense of balance. We can no longer watch and feel. Instead, we identify with those sensations, and they take over our thoughts and actions. We then try to get away, fleeing, no longer present—or we dramatize. That is why acceptance of our emotions and working through the shadows of our psyches are critical to the spiritual path. We develop a stability of mind, like a deeply rooted tree that can weather the wind.

SEPARATION

As you deepen your capacity to be present to your mind's machinations and wanderings, you learn how your mind operates. You soon realize that your suffering is not limited to the traumatic traces of the past. It is also found in how you meet the present. In fact, as we will see, we suffer in the present because the present we perceive is, in truth, a version of the past recycled. Hence, to be present *to the present moment* is, paradoxically, always a confrontation with the past.

This work of being present will make apparent just how repetitive your thoughts are. You may notice that your thoughts seem to wander incessantly over the same points. They may be thoughts about other people or yourself, filled with emotional pockets, yearning, anger, frustration, resentment, envy, desire, longing, etc. You may find yourself defending yourself, wanting to be right, to be seen, to be heard, to be validated. You may find yourself wanting to escape some present condition, some circumstance in your life that you want to be different, that you want to change. You discover that you are, in a way, living in a time loop. You are experiencing your own version of *Groundhog Day*, where each day resembles the previous one.

All of these repetitive thoughts bumping around in your head almost always take the form of criticism and judgment, both of yourself and others. Judgment is the primordial programming of the ego. It is the baseline from which the ego is born and thus what it knows how to do best. This is part of what distinguishes humans from nature—we are constantly evaluating and discriminating against that which surrounds us. We distinguish ourselves in time and space—I am me, and I am here now, and you are you, and you are there now. We establish coordinates for ourselves, in time and space, in relation to each other. From there, the ego overlays everything that is separate from us with judgment. This is fundamentally what we mean when we talk about separation in the spiritual world.

Judgment here is the basic practice of deciding whether something is good or bad, whether you like it or not, or whether it should or shouldn't be. Your mind is constantly evaluating the world it experiences on some hierarchy of value, determining if there's some kind of threat or benefit to you. Judgment may seem innocuous when it simply registers as personal preference for one thing over another, but it is the structure that gives rise to views that some belong and others do not.

Judgment also relies on the mind's tendency to reduce the complexity of the world to simple binaries. The mind likes to simplify. It makes the world easier to understand and takes less energy and effort. Simplicity reigns over nuance. One of the primary ways the mind cultivates simplicity is through binary thinking. Binaries divide the world into two buckets. From there, judgment is easier: one bucket is better than the other bucket. Spend any time in the political realm, and you can see how easily this structure of thought pervades the world we live in.

When we work with binaries, we break everything down into parts that appear to be opposites but are just simplifications of the world. We tend to use binaries for most things, often when it comes to categories of identity. But the simplest ones are those that we've already touched on: me vs. you, us vs. them. Sameness and difference, right and wrong, good and bad are all versions of the same core binary of me vs. you. This same type of binary thinking plays out in categories of sexuality, race, and gender, where the mind's tendency toward binary thought reduces complexity to white vs. nonwhite, men vs. women, and gay vs. straight, even though each of those categories is infinitely more complex than the words suggest.

Even the most trivial kinds of binaries show up in the ways we like to establish rivalries between two entities. Take, for example, the state of New York vs. the state of New Jersey. Or the way rivalries develop between sports teams. Each of these is defined against the other, with one side claiming superiority. We do it with generalizations about the North vs. the South, Democrats vs. Republicans, men vs. women. Binary thinking coupled with judgment is the most common way that we carve up the world to simplify and manage it.

We do the same with events in our lives, reducing them to a binary of good or bad. The Zen parable of "Maybe" captures this dimension of our minds so succinctly. In that story, an old farmer loses his horse, and a neighbor laments his friend's bad luck. "Maybe," the farmer says in response. The horse soon returns along with several other wild ones, and the neighbor proclaims that this is good news. Again, the farmer replies, "Maybe." The farmer's son tries to ride one of the wild horses, falls, and breaks his leg. The neighbor, unable to keep his judgment to himself, again decries the farmer's bad luck. "Maybe," the farmer repeats. Military officials march into the area soon after, attempting to conscript young men for a war but bypass the son because his leg is broken. The neighbor applauds the farmer's luck, and the farmer, as you might guess, responds with "Maybe." In the face of each event, the evaluation of whether it was "good" or "bad" could not yet be seen except within a broader context of time, a context that was always shifting as time went on. The farmer embodied a sense of balance, refusing to interpret each event as bad or good.

The ego is much like the neighbor, churning out one judgment, one criticism, one superlative after another, almost always within a binary framework. So being present means watching the nonstop flow of mental activity by your mind, all of which is happening in the present moment, which might take the form of ruminating about the past or fretting about the future or simply criticizing and resisting the present moment. To be present is to be the farmer who suspends judgment. Your mind is never at rest, but constantly retelling old stories, imagining new ones, and offering some kind of interpretation of what it perceives. Being present means letting go of the need to interpret the world around you symbolically.

THE PRESENT IS THE PAST RECYCLED

By being present to your mind, you soon realize that all that passes through your mind is your perception. Here, we are going to deepen our understanding of the present moment. It is the temporal plane in which mental activity takes place. It is the only moment of time that our consciousness *experiences*. Within that plane, we have lots of thoughts about the past and the future—mental fabrications—as well as thoughts about what is happening before our very eyes. Yet the really wild truth is that what is happening before your very eyes is itself still not the present moment—it is, rather, your mental fabrication of the present moment. Take a moment to let that sink in, for it sounds paradoxical, and it is.

Your perception of the present is an illusion. Physics tells us that in fact we never see the present. The light you perceive refracted through your eyes and processed by your brain is fractions of a second old by the time that processing occurs.[5] That light is no longer in the present time of the source that emitted it; it is fractions older. "The light takes time to reach you, let's say a few nanoseconds—a tiny fraction of a second—therefore, you are not quite seeing what she is doing *now* but what she was doing a few nanoseconds ago," writes physicist Carlo Rovelli. You are always seeing the past, never the present.

You might object that this insight is important as a matter of physics, but for everyday life, a few nanoseconds probably doesn't matter that much. After all, the fractional difference in time means that, for all of us, what we call the present is virtually the same age from the perspective of physics. But this physical reality extends even further to the particular ways you've processed this imagery. For the world you perceive that is fractions of a second older is even older in psychological terms. You are seeing what you have seen through prior experiences and concepts you've gained much earlier in life. Those are unique to you. The image of the person in front of you, which physically is fractions of a second from the past, is actually a vision that you see filtered through your mind's perceptions, which are themselves rooted further in the past. We see with old eyes. We are always recycling the past in the present moment.

Put differently, everything we remember, perceive, or imagine is always happening as activity in the present, yet it is always based on what we already know. In this way, we are caught in a kind of time loop. Our past is prologue. We see now, and will see in the future, what our minds have already learned to see. In this way, what we perceive as the present moment is itself only a tiny sliver of what there is to perceive. Our minds take in that data, which we have seen before, and we now are in the realm of memory. Most of what you see is a recreation of what you have already seen. Your home, your body, your friends, your workplace—the physical world that you encounter is data that your mind has seen already. It appears that the world is constant. Instead, it is your mind conceiving of it in each instant of the now.

In each moment, then, we recreate the world. Each moment is but a snapshot of our minds' perception of reality. Yet we recreate that reality with the same images. Life looks fluid, but it's like an old-time reel of pictures, one snapshot after the other, that the mind melds together to give us a sense of continuity. The world is brand new in each instant yet looks pretty much the same, and that is because change, or entropy, is occurring constantly, albeit quite slowly by our eyes' capacity to measure that change. In this way, every moment I encounter is a new one but filtered through my memory. The changes are barely perceptible, which is why we don't notice aging from day to day, but we can notice a person has changed if we haven't seen them in years. Change—death and rebirth—happens in each and every moment.

In this way, all of us share a relationship to clock time, but we are also separate dimensions of time. Each of us perceives the world as separate from us, and we are never able to inhabit or understand another's experience of time. We can only approximate it through the medium of language. However much we might seem to share the same space and align our lives in time, you will always see the world through your unique consciousness; what appears to you in any given moment is a world I will not experience. I will experience my own version of the world, and you will experience yours. But my perception and your perception will never be fully shared. We can at most approximate each other's perceptions. Even if we converge at the same time and place—getting together to watch a movie or working at the same office, for example—each of us will experience the passage of time differently. I will perceive time at the office or in the movie differently from you. That is what makes our individual consciousness separate and unique.

Everything you are perceiving as the now is a perception based on your particular past. You're perceiving based on prior experience, previously learned concepts, etc. In fact, you're producing the now as a version of your past. This applies not only to your particular judgments and criticisms, but even your mind's most neutral descriptions—the perceptions of physical reality, what you think you see, are themselves constructions. The words you use to describe the world around you, even in the most neutral or positive ways, are constructions. You perceive a chair. Is it a chair? Why is that a chair? What makes it a chair? Our eyes give us data, and we have a language for it—the word "chair." That reality itself is something of a construct. We take a dynamic and complex reality of which we can only perceive a small part, and we organize it mentally into different units and label it with words. The legs and seat of a chair form a chair; several chairs and another unit we call a table come together; they are placed in larger units we call homes; those are placed in larger units we call a neighborhood. Our minds, together with language, construct and constitute the reality we perceive. But we see, and hear, and taste, and smell only that which we have already learned. Even when we experience something new, we interpret it by analogy to the past.

Your vision of the present is both distorted in the sense

that it's really a replication of the past and partial in that there's always more you could be seeing. And even if you could see "more," it might be "new" the first time you see it, but the next time you see it, you will be seeing it through the eyes of the prior experience. In this way, you're recreating the present moment again and again, based on prior concepts. You are the past, present, and future already, in this very moment, each influencing the other. Isn't that a wild conundrum? You have to look at the world and accept that what you are seeing is not the full picture. Ask yourself instead: What else is there to see here? What am I not seeing because I am only looking at what I am used to seeing? What can't I see because I've never seen it and don't even know to look for it? What else could I see even if I have no framework or language for it?

This concept is similar to what Buddhists refer to as form-lessness, or what contemporary spirituality might call the unmanifest.[6] It is that which is beyond form. In this way, each of us takes in only a small part of the data of the world, through our senses, filtered through the constructs our minds have built out of concepts and experiences. When you become aware of your mind, you see that your mind is constantly filtering the present world around you—what you can derive in this instant from sight, sound, touch, taste, and smell—by taking in only a small portion of what's available to it. This is why we each have such different perceptions. We each take in only so much of the world as our minds allow; our memories are selective, our perceptions differ. Each of us is a version of Leonard.

* * *

When you meditate for a long while, particularly during a lengthy retreat, you can begin to slow down and see just how much information your mind filters. Slowing down often results first in boredom. The mind wants stimulation. As you continue to slow your perception of time by taking in more and more data and letting your mental judgments and evaluations of that data subside, a shift can take place. Your mind becomes less focused on analyzing what it is receiving and more focused on taking in more data. More and more of the present moment that surrounds you can be taken in through all of your senses. You can start to see how little of the world you actually allow your mind to process, because you're too busy describing, analyzing, interpreting, and criticizing the small amount you allow yourself to perceive. The more you slow down and allow the world to enter you, the more you allow the boundaries between the exterior world and your experience of it to blur.

During a nine-day silent meditation retreat, I began to slow down considerably around day six or seven. The next day I really slowed down. I began to eat my food in slow motion; my walking meditations happened in slow motion. Where I might have walked across the room in thirty seconds, I now took fifteen minutes. Because my mind had slowed down after so much silent meditation, as I slowed my movement my mind could start to take in data that it used to filter out. I began to hear sounds I was not used to hearing or hadn't noticed before, like the sound of an airplane in the distance or the subtle movement of the wind through the trees. I began to take in colors and see details my eyes usually filtered out, so that the world started to look like it was in high-definition. I realized how much more I was capable of seeing, hearing, smelling, feeling, and tasting. By connecting more deeply with reality without my mind's mental commentary about it, the reality I perceived felt more vibrant, more alive, than I had previously perceived it. The world was teeming with life, but the data was so immense, I could only process it by slowing down to allow my senses to capture it. Even then, I was still only capturing a part of reality. Our senses have limits, and our minds are still constructing what they perceive based on prior concepts. We can be more and more present to all that the present moment offers but still never quite touch it fully. It is impossible to be present to all that is "now" by perceiving more and more of it, although you *will* sense the abundance of life.

TOUCHING THE PRESENT MOMENT

When you allow time to slow, when you watch your thoughts without latching onto them, you create the conditions for your mental activity to cease for a brief instant. A wave of peace hits as a gap emerges in your thinking; there comes a moment when your thoughts subside. It might pass in the blink of an eye, and then your mind will start up again, noting with astonishment how wonderful the experience was. Your mind churns again with activity, now fixated on the gap between thoughts. It starts to scramble to get back to that state, wondering how to replicate what you did previously to stop the flow of thoughts for just a second. You cannot force the mind to cease its thinking. Its activity must subside on its own. All you can do in meditation is create the conditions that allow the mind to do so.

We have, even if for just a split second, managed to get a glimpse beyond perception. There is a moment when the mind ceases to take in the data as if it were separate from what it is perceiving and no longer registers you or the world as separate from each other. Your mind has no longer separated you in time and space. This is when you have touched the present moment directly.

I remember riding a train after a weekend of intense

spiritual work, and as I stared out the window at the landscape, I became the landscape. I was the train, the window, and the flowers passing me by. I experienced complete union in that brief moment, just for a second or two. Then the thought, "That was amazing!" suddenly popped into my mind, and the connection was over. As soon as my mind described that experience in words, I fell out of unity and back into separation, back into time and space. My awareness that "I" was having an experience meant I was no longer directly in contact with the present moment. The feeling of peace, that everything was perfect just as it is, was emblazoned in me. The moment I was able to register that the experience had lasted only a few seconds, I was back to being rooted in time and now working with memory. I registered the time of the event afterwards as brief, but during that experience of unity, I had no sense of time and no sense of self. I could only analyze the event from the perspective of my current self, rooted in time, remembering what had transpired and the feeling that it had generated in me.

That moment of contact with the world speeding by outside the train, where I was the flowers, the train, and the sunlight all at once—this is what is truly meant by being in the now. It is a glimpse of contact with a world without mental filter, without your mind situating itself in time and space. It's as if I had felt our shared connection as bends in the fabric of spacetime. Your experience with the now need not be tied to a specific practice like meditation, but that practice certainly helps. Other kinds of experience approximate it. Have you had an experience where you were deep in flow? Perhaps you were mesmerized by nature, sitting at the beach or a lake, or staring at a fire. Maybe you were immersed in music. You may have slipped out of time for a split second before your mind reoriented itself. This is not about relaxation or distraction, where time speeds up. These are profound moments when time disappears. When you truly touch the present moment, time no longer registers as a moment, but as an eternity. Time can no longer be measured.

This loss of time is the loss of a sense of a separate self.[7] This cannot be understood solely as an intellectual premise, only as an experience. This is when you are truly in the present moment. You are with the crucible in which consciousness exists, seemingly beyond the mental formulation of time as past, present, and future. You are in the tableau upon which mental activity takes place, perceiving the fabric of spacetime itself. You see that time has ceased because the mind no longer differentiates itself from the rest of the world by measuring time. Time is our mechanism of separation from all that is. When it ceases, there is also no "you" to be found. By losing track of time, you have also lost track of space, and your sense of separation from it. For a split second, you are inseparable from the rest of the world. You are all of it, in that span of the time that the mind steps out of time, until you regain the flow of time.

Your mind will marvel, as mine did, at what it has touched ever so briefly once you have reoriented in time and space. You'll find that time ceases in a way that allows you to touch something between the words that so often fill your head. When this happens, we have pulled back the veil, ever so slightly, of our consciousness. Think of the universe, of reality, as a kind of cosmic Play-Doh—the fabric of spacetime. Your mind creates an image out of that Play-Doh. That's what you've learned to perceive, with the limits of human eyes and human consciousness. You see the world as form, as concept, divided into objects, layered with interpretation and judgment. Time is part of how we perceive our relationship to those objects. Our individual mental programming shapes our perception of reality; consciousness is not entirely unique. After all, we are often in agreement about the world when we are aligned in space and time. You see a chair, and I, too, see a chair; we share the concept of "chair." Then your mind layers judgment and evaluation, good or bad, on top of that chair. You get caught up in the description and the feeling it generates in you. When our minds loosen around this perception, we can experience the fullness of the fabric of reality.

When we do this, everything takes on a sheen, a lightness, that it did not quite have before, but that you now recognize has always been there. It's as if you could start to see the energy that courses through everything. It is that which is not yet form, the energy from which all matter is made. It feels like a light, a glow, a kind of heartwarming flame that, at the moment you attempt to capture it in words, flickers and blinks out. At best, you can approximate your experience of it in words. It imparts feelings of infinity, expansion, vastness, wholeness, fullness, the absence of all questions or doubt, the feeling of completeness. Once you've touched it—and you can only truly know what it is like when you've touched it, not read about it in books—you know what it is. It needs no name, this space beyond time, but we may as well call it God or the divine.

SLIPPING OUT OF TIME

Such moments are not to be chased. They cannot be grasped. The mental activity that seeks them is, ironically, the very barrier to experiencing the present moment in that way. When such moments happen, you can consider them a sign of grace. That is not to say that they are outside us or that we have to earn them. It is simply to point out that our egos are so strong that most of our lives are not spent in such a state of connection with the world. This statement is not meant to signal failure.

On the contrary, it recognizes how powerful our minds are in constructing the world as we perceive it. If your mind is able to fall out of time even for a moment, thus allowing you to experience unity with the world, you should be grateful for such a rare experience in grace.

If this connection with reality cannot be pursued, how do you access this present moment? The spiritual path's emphasis on time offers an invitation to loosen your grip on your concepts and perceptions—and any judgments, resistance, and other emotions attached to them—because they filter the now, allowing you to see only a small portion of reality. You start by giving up the very claim to know and see the world fully. This means adopting a sense of humility at what you do perceive, because you recognize that your mind can only capture a small part of reality. It means holding your perceptions quite gently and without great attachment, because they are so partial. You can hold your concepts of what you see—and what you think of now as the truth—very lightly, because you may need to revise them, or jettison them altogether.

You'll notice how you identify people and places and meet them with your memories—seeing with old eyes—and the emotions they stir. Instead, practice seeing as if you were seeing for the first time, with no opinions or expectations. You can practice this through awareness, through meditation, through acceptance of your body and your emotions. Your judgments and emotional resistance to the present are a reflection of your past—the prior selves that you have not resolved. The more you are present to and accept your feelings, the more clearly you see your mind. You begin to perceive how your mind constantly generates categories, descriptions, and labels for different parts of the world. You become aware of how your mind then applies all sorts of judgments to different pieces of the world. When you do the work of healing the past and watching with compassion how your mind tries to carve up the world, you can hold those concepts more lightly. You find yourself at peace because you no longer hold onto your mind's evaluations as truth.

As you dive deeper into your psyche, accepting with compassion your mind's unique way of perceiving the world, your mind's need to separate itself from the rest of the world will relax on its own. Your mind's sense of vigilance, built around fear of difference and threats, will subside. Memory will still exist, as you'll see the world and perceive the data of the world as you previously did. But you will need not so easily impose your prior experiences, particularly your emotional reactivity, on any particular person or object. You will hold your concepts and memories a bit more lightly. You will soon loosen your penchant for judgment. You will see the world a bit more brightly, because it will seem newer and more alive. Everything will appear less shrouded in your judgments than before. There's a natural beauty that begins to emerge beyond the veil of the mind's descriptors. The world will seem more alive to you because you will have caught a glimpse of the spirit that courses through all of reality. You'll see the world more clearly as movements of the fabric of spacetime. You'll feel more easily how we are all part of that same fabric. From a spiritual perspective, you'll see the divine energy that flows through all creation, beyond words and beyond time, to peek through the forms and objects of the world.

As your practice deepens, your perception may evolve. I experienced a radical shift in perception in 2014: I started to see cascading showers of light. I was staring at the floor of a hotel room, and this thought passed through my mind in a split second: "It's raining." But I was staring at the floor, and what my mind initially took as the kind of misty droplets you might see when you first emerge from the shower or a sauna were instead fast-moving streaks of light. I've never stopped seeing that light. It's one of the most wondrous experiences of my life: I started to see a part of the "now" my mind had never before permitted me to see. My consciousness shifted to allow my mind to perceive a different level of data than it did before, but my mind still perceived the data of the physical universe in some way.

A similar experience occurred when I was on ayahuasca, when I stepped out in the moonlight and saw the jungle. I saw it through new eyes: vibrating, glowing, teeming with life my normal senses could not perceive. That is not to say that I saw nature "as it truly is," for there is no singular "reality" that "is." There is no reality that we can all agree on, only the reality that each of us perceives through our consciousness. Instead, I glimpsed the wonder of nature through a different consciousness, one that allowed me to recognize that my prior perception was very limited. The experience left me quite humbled, knowing just how little of nature I truly perceive.

The spiritual path is not about eschewing the past or avoiding the future so that you face only what is directly in front of you. You go about your life, orienting yourself in time and space, including turning to the future. It is a helpful reminder that Zen temples do not ignore clock time. They have calendars for meditation, dharma talks, and meals. Assistants to the Zen priests ring bells in the morning to awaken the residents for the first meditation session of the day. The same is true for contemporary spiritual teachers who espouse the now; surely, they have calendars, plan talks, and announce events in the future.[8] If you're planning a trip, with all of the future-oriented aspects like dates for your flight and hotel room, you do so without the anxiety that something will go wrong. You don't make plans to flee the present moment, hoping that vacation will give you peace. You plan a vacation because it is a wonderful experience to have that requires you to coordinate with others (hotels, airlines, etc.). You meet that mental activity in the present moment without resistance, and if emotional energy arises, you meet that too.

Yet you do all of this with the awareness that you are witnessing your perception and that what you are seeing is but a sliver of the reality beyond form—another way of referring to the divine. The possibility and promise of the unknown, of the unseen, should give rise instead to wonder and excitement. Awe arises because you actually don't see all there is to see, you don't hear all there is to hear, and you don't feel all there is to feel. The mystery of reality is right there, barely perceptible to you, in this very moment. The wonder and mystery of the world will never cease and can never be fully grasped. Instead, you realize that there is a kind of pleasure to be found in accepting that you can never fully perceive all there is in the present moment. You can meet the present moment with a willingness to see more or see differently than you did before, and that gives rise to a sense of wonder. As you expand your capacity to see what is there and what is possible, you also accept that what you are seeing is just a piece of a totality that you'll never fully grasp. The world will always hold some mystery, something new and unknown, to share with you. In that way, we can experience time, from moment to moment, without attempting to achieve some kind of blissful dissolution into divine ecstasy. We can experience each moment of our seemingly ordinary, mundane lives with this sense of wonder. We don't need to see our daily moments as lacking or unsatisfactory compared to some state of altered consciousness.

This last point is critical, for we are not meant to live with each other in that blissful space of union. We can sometimes turn that experience into a pursuit; we judge our everyday experiences as lacking compared to the bliss of the eternal now. It implies that we fail if we perceive the world as we did before, and not as some shimmering mirage filled with light. This is not a failure. The goal of spirituality is not to have our consciousness dissolve in this kind of "now," where we live in timelessness. That is often how the contemporary emphasis on the present moment is received, as if you were making a mistake if you're not sitting in bliss, oblivious to the passage of time, in every instance of your life. Instead, the path is to embrace the paradox that we are simultaneously bound by time and able to fall out of it.

We must live in time together. You can touch the timeless, and then your mind will reorient itself in time. You might touch it for a moment, or even become immersed in the bliss for longer than a second. You will then reorient in time and space. Perception, concepts, and memory will resume. You will coordinate your life with others. The moment you think and speak, the moment your mind resumes its perception, you are no longer immersed in the present. You are present to whatever arises, without expectation of some altered or heightened state of consciousness. When we embrace this movement in and out of time wholeheartedly, time becomes a portal to a life of peace and happiness. Every moment offers an opportunity to release our separation and be present to all that is right now. The world shimmers a bit more brightly the more you are willing to take it in, just as it is.

ENERGY:
YOU ARE AS TIMELESS AS THE COSMOS

How many times have you stood outside on a clear night, staring up at the sky, in awe at the vastness of the universe? You might have felt a sense of wonder at the mystery of the universe we occupy and how little we understand of it. You might have even fallen out of time, ever so briefly. You might have felt intrigued to know that the light you see coming through those stars is millions of years old, having originated so long ago that the stars that emitted it might not even exist anymore. The universe that erupted from the Big Bang represents an expanse of time and space that our minds struggle to comprehend.

That sense of intrigue and wonder at the infinite reaches of the universe, and how little we know of it, might then shade into an appreciation of our smallness. You might reflect on how, in the depth of time and space, each of us is just a small speck of stardust, gone in nearly an instant. Like the tiny cells that make up our body, whose time is but a small fraction of our lifespan, so too are we infinitesimal when compared to the time span of the universe. It is often a humbling act to be reminded of how transient our time is here on the planet. That awareness can sometimes help us to appreciate the here and the now, to separate the trivial from what truly matters to us.

If we are not inspired to feel awe and wonder, our smallness and fragility in a physical world might instead give birth to insecurity. We may feel vulnerable to threats on a physical level, and on an emotional level, we may feel trivial or irrelevant. We wonder if we have a purpose and question the meaning of life. Our status as specks of stardust can move from a sense of majesty at being part of a creation that is almost incomprehensible to a profound anxiety about our place in it. Our minds, overwhelmed by this state of affairs, may reach the dubious conclusion that we really don't matter.

Just as we are inseparable from the natural world, so too are we inseparable from the cosmos. We are made of the same material as the sun, the moon, and the stars. We are stardust from the Big Bang. We are the light of distant galaxies. We are the cosmic energies flowing through the universe, unseen yet undeniable. When we are born, we have no understanding of our relationship to the physical world that our senses provide us. We are slowly inculcated into an understanding of who we are, sharing the consciousness of our fellow human beings who also see themselves as tiny specks of carbon-based life. We forget that we are as timeless as the universe itself, made up of energy that is beyond time and space.

In the face of this existential predicament, some of us attempt to expand our footprint and grow larger. We seek to build empires. Expansion and possession become the antidotes to feeling small and trivial. We amass vast sums of wealth, build brands and names, and strive for accomplishment so that we will be remembered. We attempt to ward off the feeling that our lives are meaningless and inconsequential by staking a claim to being special. If we can acquire a lot of materiality or achieve recognition, we somehow escape, if only temporarily, the transitory nature of our lives.

There is another way through this conundrum. Rather than

growing larger to avoid feeling inconsequential, we can unlearn our limited mental picture of who we are and recognize that we are not separate from the universe. We saw this already in the previous chapter, where we learned that we could fall out of time into union with reality—what it means to be truly in the present moment. Rather than seek outward expansion as a solution to our human condition, we can turn inward and discover that the universe outside mirrors the vastness of our inner worlds. As Neil deGrasse Tyson puts it, "We do not simply live in this universe. The universe lives within us."[1] When we turn inward, we begin the wondrous journey to that part of us beyond all language and beyond the body. We connect with the cosmic energy, the divine light, that shines through every one of us. We find true expansion and connection, not by amassing control over the material world, but by deepening our knowledge of the unseen and inner world. Paradoxically, the deeper we go within, the more expansive we become.

EGO EXPANSION

The path of outward expansion is one that almost everyone takes in some measure. It is the path of desire, to grow and expand, to accumulate. We counter our feelings of being small by gaining fame, followers, money, and material goods. In this way, the ultrawealthy, with vast estates and countless rooms, are no different than hoarders with modest homes filled with bags and boxes of collected items. It is an effort to fill a void.

Fame is by far the most common means of expanding the ego. Little wonder that celebrities fascinate the public, and countless people flock to Hollywood in the hopes of being "discovered." Social media now offers the promise that anybody can become an "influencer," with YouTube and Instagram helping to expand one's reach, opening us to a much larger universe of people than our family, friends, neighbors, and coworkers. So, too, is the world of business the terrain of empire builders who seek to acquire other companies, produce more products, hire more employees, and make more money.

My path until my spiritual awakening was driven by ego expansion. My preferred method of expansion was becoming smarter and more educated. I went from earning a PhD and teaching at a prestigious university in Chicago to earning a JD and clerking with prestigious judges in New York. Prestige and a career that had more influence drove me. I hungered to become a Supreme Court clerk and to teach law at a prestigious law school. As a student of cultural theory, I understood that the world was socially constructed, and law played a part in that construction. But having spurned God as a child, I did not believe that there was anything like a divine power. My worldview was that all we could do was our best to make the world a bit better through legislation, litigation, and education. I later learned that my perspective was woefully limited.

There is nothing wrong with pursuing these activities. Law, business, and entertainment are all creative enterprises. The problem is when they are pressed into the service of healing a void that cannot be healed through power, fame, or fortune. For what the ego misunderstands—indeed, cannot understand—is the fundamental nature of desire. The ego takes this existential angst about being a tiny speck of stardust and attempts to fill that emotional void with expansion. It sees the external world and *desires* it. Desire drives us to seek out fame and fortune, only to discover that fame and fortune don't fulfill us.

"If you can get this one shiny object, you will finally be happy" is the siren song of the ego. It is, of course, a lie. How many people have sought fame and fortune, only to discover that millions of fans or dollars do not in any way fill the void inside? How many have pursued relationship after relationship in the hopes of finding "the one" who would dispel the loneliness and internal ache for connection? Desire, in this form, is an appetite that can never be satiated.

In different ways, the Buddha and Freud both explained that desire is not meant to be satisfied. It is meant to be temporarily sated so that the cycle of desire, satisfaction, and desire's return can be repeated. We are compelled to restart our efforts to satiate our desire. Our desire acts almost like a time loop. Pursuing the satisfaction of desire leaves you feeling a kind of emptiness, a yearning for more. Desire itself isn't the problem—we all have desires. Rather, the problem lies in the belief that *fulfilling* your desires will alleviate that deeper sense of emptiness.

When the pursuit of desire is all that you know, you may feel still out of touch with your true self. You may feel a kind of malaise, a sense that you do not fit in the world—or you may feel simply listless. Despite the initial rush of "retail therapy," you may find yourself staring at your latest purchase with a sense of boredom or emptiness. The pursuit of the external world no longer fulfills because you are yearning to connect with your essence, your soul. This is why certain kinds of success—awards, honors, medals, titles, victories—ultimately become addictive. The high wears off, and you need another hit of worldly affirmation.

It is often through meditation that you discover this machinery of desire and dissatisfaction in your mind. Through my meditation practice, I could see my mind's machinations at work: the incessant desire to be admired for my intelligence, seen as having authority, and free from the criticisms of others. I suffered from deep-seated anxiety about the future and my place in the world. I felt a longing for connection, but I didn't know how to really open up to others. I felt a certain generalized paranoia that I might make a mistake and derail my life, the kind of error that sends you spiraling into homelessness. I numbed myself constantly with television and baked goods. Meditation helped me to see my mind and notice what I was thinking, but truth be told, even after meditating for a while, I still felt I was pretty much the same person. I was simply better at managing it. I still yearned to know myself on a much deeper level.

WE ARE ENERGY

It has become commonplace in spiritual communities to speak of energy, vibration, and frequency. Spirituality recognizes that you are animated by a living force, but what it means by these terms isn't always clear. At the level of physics, we know that everything is energy. We're made up of molecules that are made up of atomic structures composed of subatomic particles. On an anatomical level, electrical currents run through our bodies, synapses fire, and our bodies generate lots of heat. We are composed of the same elements as the sun and the stars. We are products of the energy that exploded and created the Big Bang, sending massive amounts of mass and light from the tiniest of spaces. We are part of the very fabric of spacetime, made up of particles just like the rest of the universe.

That is not normally what we mean by "energy" in the spiritual context. The energy that our bodies hold is vaster than we realize. We tap into this inherent energy when we love and accept our pain and our bodies. It is the energy we access when we inhabit the eternal present, slipping out of clock and psychological time. This energy is beyond personality and identity. This is the part that we feel strained to capture in words. It is not unique to any of us. It is not a property that can be claimed by one and denied to another. It is the spark of God within us.

This energy may very well be the energy of the stars, for when you access it, it feels cosmic. My access to this energy, which jolted me out of my ego's dissatisfaction and into connection with my soul, began with an act of grace. A series of mystical experiences erupted in my life, convulsing me out of my rational consciousness. Teachers, healers, gurus, and psychics suddenly began to show up in my life.[2] These were all individuals with the power to read and manipulate energy in ways I had never experienced. They could see my aura or energy field, and they could fill it with an energy—a feeling of bliss, lightness, and warmth—I had never experienced. They showed me that my understanding of what it means to be human was woefully limited to seeing my body solely as a physical form. All of my knowledge of language, literature, and law did little to prepare me for what more there was to see.

Our bodies are vessels for an energy that borders on celestial. You can call it the divine, the soul, or spirit. My initial encounters with this energy led me to a singular experience that revealed to me how much energy is stored within us: I experienced the awakening of my *kundalini*. In Hinduism, kundalini is the dormant spiritual energy at the base of the spine. It is often depicted as a coiled serpent in deep sleep because most people never experience its awakening. When it is awakened, through spiritual practices or divine grace, the serpent uncoils and travels up the spine—or, more accurately, an energetic channel along the spine known as the *sushumna.* As it travels upwards, the kundalini passes through each of the energetic portals known as the *chakras.* The chakras are traditionally described as energetic spheres or vortexes that correlate with specific locations on the body.

It was 2016, and I was facing the third day of rather intense lower back pain. No amount of pain reliever or stretching offered much relief. Frustrated, I lay down, attempting to relax into the pain. As I did, my lower back exploded. It felt like a hot coal smoldering at the bottom of a charcoal pit had suddenly been doused with lighter fluid. I had never experienced anything like it, even though by now I had experienced many kinds of energetic transmissions. It was a searing hot energy—almost painful—and it felt like the base of my spine had burst into flames.

The energy was so intense that my back arched. I could feel the heat pouring out from the base of my spine. This ball of electric energy moved out of the base of my spine and then paused at each of my chakra centers. It felt as though the energy was expanding at each chakra, pushing those energy centers open, removing obstacles and blockages in its path.

Sometimes the process was quite electric, hot, and even painful, causing me to break into a sweat. Other times, it was soothing, smooth, and even blissful. I also experienced *kriyas*, which are spontaneous movements in which the body shakes and spasms as the kundalini moves through. This energy emanated from within. It did not feel like it came from an exterior source, but as if it came from some higher realm. Yet it did not feel like any kind of internal sensation I had ever experienced. It felt like it was bursting forth from the core of my being.

The kundalini had an agenda all of its own, but I never felt afraid that I was somehow in danger, as if any harm would come from this experience. On the contrary, I was often in a state of bliss as the kundalini moved through me. Despite its intensity, I understood that this was one of the most loving and transformative experiences available to a human being.

The traditional model tells us that each chakra relates to an area of human life. The root chakra, located near the base of your spine, relates to safety and security, such as having your body's basic needs met. The sacral chakra, located below the belly button, relates to creativity, sexuality, and relationships. The solar plexus chakra, located a few inches above your belly button, relates to willpower, identity, and your sense of self. The heart chakra relates to your capacity to give and receive love. The throat chakra is the seat of expression—your capacity to voice your needs and share your thoughts. The third eye, located in the space between your eyebrows, is the seat of your imagination, intuition, and intellectual inspiration. The crown chakra at the top of your head relates to your connection to your soul, a higher power, and consciousness itself.

We think that our bodies are matter, but they are also energetic fields where so much of our emotional energy is stored. I experienced these chakras as discrete spheres, each linked to the next one, in succession, from the base of the spine to the crown of the head. But I learned from this experience that there are lines of connection between one or more chakras relating to specific traumatic events, limiting beliefs, emotional patterns, and past life karma.

Betrayal by a loved one, for example, won't affect just the heart chakra. A thread might be woven through the sacral chakra and the heart chakra. If that betrayal affects your material well-being, like being kicked out of your home and having no job, the emotional pain will likely be linked to your root chakra. Your sense of self might also be harmed, causing the thread to wind through your solar plexus. If you find you can't speak about your pain because you are so ashamed or hurt, your throat chakra might also be impacted. Beliefs, thoughts, and emotions around a particular event or person relate to multiple areas of your life, and thus there are multiple threads woven through different chakra points.

Nor does the energy limit itself to the chakras. The kundalini goes deep into the bones, muscles, and organs. I've felt the energy penetrate different parts of my physical body, which were also holding deeply embedded fears and other strong emotions, so that the energy could be released. Not all of this has been blissful either. Opening some parts of those chakras or certain areas of my body has led me to the deepest pits of despair, conjuring up profoundly sad, bitter, or angry energy, connected with bleak thoughts. The deeper you go, the denser the shadows.

The healing energy I experienced was not directed solely at releasing and cleansing old wounds. The power of the kundalini also awakened in me psychic faculties that had been dormant. A month into the experience, I began to receive downloads of spiritual wisdom, what is commonly known as channeling. Now, when I work with clients, I receive downloads of information about their lives and karmic history in the same way, in what is known as clairaudience or claircognizance.

The energy still moves through me almost daily; after so many years, the intensity ebbs and flows. The energy sometimes begins as kundalini, at the base of the spine. Other times, it begins as cosmic energy, through the crown chakra, as I feel light pouring into the top of my head. Either one often leads me to a state of bliss, of divine union, called *samadhi* or *satori*. This is a point of cosmic union where you recognize that you are not separate from the universe. Rather, spacetime is something we experience as part of our consciousness. It is here that I know that each of us is timeless, that we are souls who do not follow the dictates of linear time, even as our unenlightened minds do.

PAST LIVES AND GENERATIONAL KARMA

My kundalini awakening taught me that our bodies are vast repositories of emotional energy, but that they contain far more than we can imagine. The healing was not limited to the patterns and pain that I associate with my life in this body during this lifetime. It went even deeper. The notion of reincarnation and past lives has long been a source of dispute in the realm of religion and spirituality. Some traditions have long espoused the idea that we are born again and again; others have said that we are lucky to have had a single human birth and will need to accrue significant amounts of good karma to enjoy another one. Once again, my mystical experiences with both divine energy and plant medicine confirmed that our bodies are vast repositories of time and emotional energy. We house within us stores of past life memories and unresolved pain.

During these kundalini episodes, I have released energy from my body that was not "mine" in the sense that I could not tie it to a particular episode of my life. Instead, I was flooded with memories and emotions that felt like they belonged to someone else. Empaths often feel other people's emotions and recognize that they are not our own. Similarly, I've felt eruptions of pain and energy in different parts of my body or in different chakras where, suddenly, memories and emotions from lives I do not remember flooded my mind; I experienced over and over again residual feelings and emotions from those past experiences until the chakra and the body parts associated with the energy were finally cleared.

Understanding how deeply embedded these energies were and where they came from helped me understand why these emotional patterns had been so deeply entrenched in my life and psyche, and why they had remained immune to traditional therapy or even meditation. Each chakra is an almost endless storage unit of psychic residues, memories, and emotions. In a word, all of us are walking around with storehouses of trauma passed down through time—a reality that the fields of psychology and neuroscience are now beginning to understand as inherited, generational trauma.[3] You are the dreams of your ancestors, but you have also carried for them their nightmares so that you might unburden them.

My experience is consistent with shamanic traditions that also see the body as containing much negative energy that must be purged and eliminated. A similar experience occurred while I was on ayahuasca. Shortly after I downed the potent brew, the hallucinogenic fireworks began, and I started to writhe, moving back and forth. My body convulsed in a strange, almost animal-like fashion. I had two enormous purges and then felt nothing but sheer agony throughout my entire body. The pain was physical and emotional. Nothing made it go away, and the ayahuasca kept repeating the word *somete*—Spanish for *surrender*.

As I reached out for one of the assistants to ask why the ayahuasca wasn't talking to me and why I was in so much pain, the plant medicine took all language away from me, and I couldn't speak. After what felt like an eternity, the pain slowly began to shift. The message became clear: I was feeling, and thereby releasing, pain carried in my body from previous lifetimes. It was most intense around my belly button, as if I were feeling the pain of death and rebirth again and again. Slowly, over the next couple of hours, I went through a complete rebirth and received the gift of language again. The next day, I spoke with the shamans who had overseen the ceremony, and they told me that I was now like a spiritual newborn, a young child delivered back to a state of innocence. I had purged countless volumes of unresolved generational and past-life trauma.

THE UNIVERSE IS MADE OF LOVE, AND SO ARE YOU

These mystical adventures might suggest that we are endless repositories of pain. But that would be a bleak and partial view of what we are. If we are countless lifetimes of unresolved memory and emotion, we are also countless lifetimes of joy and love. We are a mix of pleasure and pain. Eons of intimacy, affection, and happiness from our ancestors, all of whom experienced both joy and pain, flow through the genetic material of our bodies. We are still filled with scary moments, but also moments of love. Every moment of joy, wonder, and happiness is also with you, along with all the sadness, anger, and fear. Times when your father ignored you, your mother criticized you, your siblings made fun of you, your father left, your mother wasn't able to love you in the way you wanted, your heart was broken by your first love, your best friend moved away, you got a bad grade, a friend was mean to you, you didn't get something you really wanted—are all within you.

It's true that all of that energy is there. But it rests alongside the energy of your first kiss, the time you won an award— or got a good grade, or made a new friend, or fell down and scraped your leg and your mother comforted you, or ate pizza with friends until your stomach ached, or spent slumber parties playing tricks, or ate treats with your grandmother that your mother would disapprove of. All of your interactions, positive and negative, are stored in your body and memories, even if you're not conscious of them. Collectively, that energy, positive and negative, is with you each and every moment.

Our conventional perception of our bodies as physical entities is only part of the picture. In the language of physics, we are both wave and particle. The energy that enters my crown chakra or erupts from my root chakra is unlike anything I've experienced. This experience of energy can last for hours; it's as if I were plugged into a cosmic electrical outlet. I'm often still aware of time and my body, but I am filled with energy, like a balloon of light. Whether the energy feels burning or soothing, it leaves me with a feeling of complete peace and unconditional love. It fills me with a profound reverence for life. I see the world, and it is in perfect, divine order.

You need not chase states of consciousness like the ones that I have described here. They cannot be forced; they are a form of divine grace. You don't need to have the blissful experience of *samadhi* or *satori* to understand that you are divine. If you experience them, you'll feel a sense of grace and you'll understand experientially, not intellectually, what it means to feel connected to the cosmos. But your divinity is already there, in your capacity to give and receive love, to meet the world with compassion and gratitude. The path is to remind yourself through practice and devotion that the universe is made of love, and so are you.

You can cultivate and deepen your capacity to love, to broaden your heart and therefore feel more compassion and acceptance in each moment. You can tap into this cosmic energy of love woven into the very fabric of spacetime to feel more connected to the divine.

Spiritual tools like meditation continue to create the space of awareness so that you can face and meet your thoughts and emotions wholeheartedly. In that way, you strengthen your compassion for yourself. A particularly powerful practice for opening your heart is to meditate on all the people who have loved you and you love in return—be they parents, partners, relatives, friends, or children. You can include those who have taken care of you, like nannies, teachers, doctors and nurses, or mentors of some kind. Simply call to mind all of the people who have made a positive contribution to your life. Another meditation practice is called *metta*, or lovingkindness, in which you cultivate a positive mindset and wishes for happiness for different people, including those whom you find challenging or difficult to be around.[4]

You can also cultivate a sense of reverence for the divine, in whatever form most speaks to you. This can include reverence for nature or prayer to the divine. Having a regular practice of connecting with God, in whatever way resonates most deeply for you, is an integral part of the path. Chanting mantras or singing devotional songs, such as kirtan, are also powerful tools. Gratitude for what you have in your life instills a sense of appreciation and dispels lack so that you see the bounty already existing around you. You can simply set the intention to connect with your soul or feel your inherent connection to the divine. The energy of that intention plants a seed in your heart that will ultimately grow into a deep trust that the divine is already inside you.

Connect with what inspires you at the level of your soul. What do you love to do? What sparks joy for you? Spend time connecting with the people in your life who are the most reliable sources of love and comfort. What makes you feel alive? Do those activities with abandon, without pretense of needing to justify them. Read works of spiritual wisdom that you find uplifting. Set an intention each day to connect with God and ask to see the world through the eyes of the divine. Ask to experience the feeling of unconditional love. Ask for your soul to show you who you truly are and allow what shows up to speak to you.

LOVING OUR STATE OF SEPARATION

Even if I feel divine, cosmic energy through these experiences, I cannot live in a state of divine union. I must return to time and space, to interactions with my fellow human beings. Even if you feel that you're moving in perfect concert with the cosmos, you will discover that you do not always see our perfectly imperfect world through the eyes of love. This connection to a divine love that asks nothing and gives everything is always available to us, even if it often feels elusive. We might touch it once and then find ourselves struggling to regain that sense of peace. We might touch it regularly but find that our inner connection with the divine is easily shaken by external events and conflicts with others.

We might ask ourselves why we don't feel the spark of God inside of us all the time. Why can't we feel love and only love? Why can't we live in divine bliss? This is where it is important to cultivate this sense of acceptance and compassion for all that arises within you. For all too often, spiritual seekers will begin to feel more and more blissful states as they feel more awakened. As you meditate, pray, engage in rituals, undertake adventures in plant medicine or reiki or other forms of energy healing, as you chant mantras or sing kirtan, as you connect with your soul, you can fall into an expectation of constant happiness. You fall into the trap of toxic positivity where every instance of negative emotion, every hint of an older version of yourself, every indication that you are falling into a conventional way of seeing the world is a sign of failure. You reproach yourself and resist these moments as signs that your frequency has dropped. You're in a state of vigilance, seeing the world as a constant symbolism of your consciousness.

But if my experiences in consciousness can speak to

anything universal, it is that we are an amalgam of so much unresolved emotional energy, there is not a single frequency at which we are vibrating. It is not the emotion or mental belief system or self-limiting block that reflects our state of alignment with our soul. It is, rather, our willingness to remain present to and compassionate with ourselves in these moments of purported shortcoming. These are moments when we can recognize that we have fallen back into the traps of desire, attachment, and identity by clinging to a particular energetic state. We start to form attachments to certain emotions or states, such as bliss or peace or joy, and we fall back into the old human pattern of wanting to avoid discomfort and pain. We start to form an identity around our spiritual path, telling ourselves that this is the path of freedom from pain.

Freedom is found not when you are somehow free of pain, but rather when you are free of suffering. That happens when you embrace the truth that your healing journey knows no end. As we saw in the first chapter, we release the perception that our pain is a wound to be healed rather than a portal to greater light. There will not be any point in a human body where you can entirely escape time and space. You will have more challenges, you will feel negative emotions, and you will fall back into separation. Having "negative" experiences or emotions is not a sign that your frequency is "low." This is an all-too-common idea in the spiritual world. Resisting those experiences or blaming yourself for your supposedly low frequency is what characterizes a "low frequency." Be aware when your mind wants to push these events out of your consciousness and blames you for what has transpired. Your frequency is measured by your resistance to these moments where some old pain or pattern comes back up for healing. Your frequency is measured by your capacity to remain aligned with your soul and in balance even in those most demanding of challenges. Can you still see everything and everybody through the eyes of God, through the eyes of love, even if you are also at the same time feeling immense pain?

That is what it means to remain in a high state of consciousness. It is not the absence of negativity. It is the absence of resistance to negativity. And even when you feel resistance, you then must step back and be compassionate to yourself for feeling this resistance—for this, too, is a normal part of the spiritual journey. You will hold this part of you that is in resistance, that doesn't want to sit and listen to your sadness or anxiety but would prefer to numb itself. You will hold yourself gently when you go ahead and choose to numb yourself and later want to reproach yourself for not doing what you "should" have done instead.

This is the art of being a divine human. It is the incremental work of aligning yourself with your heart and soul, from moment to moment. It is learning to love even when we aren't in a state of divine bliss. The path is to see each moment as an opportunity to deepen our capacity to love. Cultivating that space of love and compassion, the place where we feel whole and alive, requires a kind of dedication that is both tender and strong at the same time. Every time you see your pain with compassion, you've tapped once again the cosmic energy of unconditional love. That energy can never be lost. It is part of the very fabric of your being.

FINDING A TEACHER

What that means, ultimately, is that this journey is yours alone to navigate. You are your own universe, and only you can chart it. That does not mean, as many assume, that teachers don't exist, or that you already have all the answers to all the questions.

In the contemporary spiritual world, the pendulum has swung in the other direction and there is now widespread rejection of authority. That is a mistake. It misunderstands the role of the teacher because we have treated teachers, gurus, and religious figures in a way that has undermined that inner journey to our own cosmic knowledge. Teachers, healers, and guides are here to facilitate and accelerate your journey. Throughout our history, though, we have tended to privilege certain types of figures as mediators for the divine, those who are anointed to speak to God on our behalf. We have gone in search of God through emissaries, treating the divine as always outside of us, at a distance that can only be bridged by another. We seek out gurus whom we follow, and as the history of gurus suggests, this phenomenon often leads to scandal and abuse.

The true guru exists to model for you that the divine is inside each of us. An authentic teacher has the capacity to brighten that light inside us, to lift some of the layers that cloak it, because they understand that we are all divine. They can awaken the energy we have inside that is blocked by our minds and our unresolved emotions. When we see the guru as the incarnation of the divine, we are not meant to see ourselves as lesser than them, as if they were connected to the divine and we were not. On the contrary, they are here to demonstrate that we are just like them. The true guru doesn't ask you to prostrate before them as a substitute for God. The true teacher does not demand loyalty, subordination, or obeisance. The true guru teaches you to see them, one human being, as divine. The problem is when we forget the next step: that we should see *every* human being as divine, not just the guru or teacher. You are God; so is the teacher; and so is everyone else.

Navigating our way through our internal world to find the divine inside often depends, paradoxically, on teachers and guides who can walk alongside us, accompanying us as we make our way to this inner truth. After all, if you are the universe, and that teacher has shown up, they are a part of you. They are simply appearing in the external world as a reflection of some inner knowing deep inside you. Your wisdom often needs to circumvent the conscious mind, which cannot always heal itself of the trauma and suffering you've endured. Your mind might be too blocked for you to access your internal wisdom. In that case, rather than show up as an inner voice or knowledge, your wisdom appears in the form of an external guide, teacher, book, or event. Your soul conjures forth what you need when you are ready, in divine timing. Those teachers share their light with us when ours is dimmed by the emotional weight of our past and the limitations of our current consciousness. They kindly extend us a flashlight to help us illuminate the path as we chart our own course to our soul.

IDENTITY:

YOU ARE A WORLD BEYOND WORDS

How many times have you looked at your life and questioned whether this is who you are and where you were supposed to be? These are the questions prompted by our soul or our spirit, the part of us that is wise, whole, and loving. In Paolo Coelho's popular tale, *The Alchemist*, the protagonist Santiago pursues these very questions when he embarks on a quest to fulfill his purpose—what he calls his "personal legend." Prompted by a dream of buried treasure, he sets out in search of it, aided along the way by numerous figures. It is a tale of a shepherd who yearns to know his soul and fulfill his purpose for being here.

It is only at the end of his journey, however, that he discovers that what he was seeking was with him from the very beginning—the buried treasure was in the very spot where he began his journey. The journey to both the soul and the buried treasure required what seemed like an external voyage but was in reality an unwinding of his ways of seeing himself and the world. As he took an outer voyage, he was also engaged in an inner voyage of self-discovery that allowed him to unlock his truth.

Each of us is a constellation of emotions, thoughts, and beliefs. Each of us has a body that seems material but is also full of energy that reflects our inherent connection to the divine. We cannot escape clock time, yet we will live in our own world of psychological time. If we are all the same in those respects, what does it mean to have an identity, a sense of self, a "personal legend," if you will, separate from everyone else?

Each of us, in one way or another, desires to become a fully realized individual, unique in some respects and different from others. We ask what our purpose is and what we are meant to do. We pursue the authentic expression of our being. We ask ourselves, *Are we a shepherd or an alchemist?*

We believe that we have a core self, an authentic identity, and that if we keep searching, eventually we'll unravel the mystery of who we are. Like the protagonist of *The Alchemist*, we'll discover our "personal legend" and know how to fulfill it. Yet during our journey through life we lay claim to many identities or roles, whether these are categories like race, gender, and sexual orientation—or professions like being a doctor, lawyer, actor, athlete, or author—or roles like being a father, or mother, or spouse. We can also lay claim to certain aspects of our personality, like whether we are introverted or extroverted. We can even lay claim to spiritual identities, choosing to present ourselves as an empath, intuitive, or healer. Who we claim to be has many facets.

When we claim an identity, we assert a sense of self that orients us in relation to the rest of the world. Those who have devoted themselves to the study of what it means to have an identity often point to how that self is never quite fixed but always in flux. Whether drawing from spirituality, psychology, cultural studies, or philosophy, the self is a complex array of identifications that are under constant reevaluation and vigilance. We are never as fixed as we might want to be. Nor are we solely the products of our own design. We inherit characteristics and are enmeshed in a cultural construct whose categories of identity precede us. The bricks we use to build the houses of our identity were not always crafted or chosen by us.

Even if identity is this ever-changing construct, you can often *feel* when you are in alignment with an authentic side of yourself. You know how it feels to feel alive and inspired in connection with your soul. You also know how it feels to be out of integrity or inauthentic, choosing to be someone you know you are not, to satisfy the wishes of others or gain approval. There's a part of you that feels more real than other parts of you, which you recognize to be holdovers from prior stages of your life. You outgrow older versions of yourself, and yet there's still some sense of inner identity that remains intact and pure. We strive to reconcile our outer identity with this inner sense of self.

We thus find ourselves at an impasse, caught between these two impulses—on the one hand, the desire to know and express our authentic self, who we feel we "really" are, and on the other, the desire to embrace an ever-changing self, in constant dialogue with the world around us, consisting of multiple identifications. If we are wave and particle, if we are a physical being and an eternal spirit, what does it mean to have an identity? Is it enough to say that we're all spiritual beings having a human experience?

There is a different way of seeing our contradictory efforts at defining ourselves. Rather than doubling our efforts to find and secure a fixed, authentic self, or rejecting any identity as just an illusion, we can learn to live within this intersection between two poles—the desire to be seen and know ourselves, on the one hand, and on the other, the truth that we are always more than our identities can ever encompass. It is in that interstice that we are able to move past the ways identities constrain us to achieve the unity that so often eludes us.

WHAT IS IDENTITY?

To understand what it means to stand at the intersection of this contradiction and to embrace it as a new way of being a spiritual self, we need to step back and look at how we come to see ourselves as a self that goes in search of an identity.

As we saw in Chapter 3 on time, our most basic sense of self comes from a consciousness that recognizes we are separate from each other in time and space. Your consciousness looks at the world in this way: *I am me and not you, now and in the next second, I am still me and you are still you, and I am still not you, and vice-versa.* What I am calling separation is simply this sense of being a singular being in time and space whose existence lies apart from the existence of all other things we perceive in the material universe. I am not this chair or this computer, as I sit typing these words. I have boundaries, and I can persist in one place, and you, the reader, in another, and we both exist even without awareness of the other.

These conditions give rise to our sense of individuality and free will, some of the most prized aspects of being human. The idea of total conformity, at least in the United States, is associated with totalitarianism. In the realm of science fiction, *Star Trek* presented this same kind of conformity through the Borg, a cyborg civilization in which each individual's consciousness was subsumed into the collective so that they were one singular entity. As presented in *Star Trek*, this was a terrifying loss of individuality and free will.

From here springs our desire for individuation, to craft an

identity, a self whose boundaries are distinct from everyone else. This is not an impulse to be disdained or rejected. To claim one's sense of self is a powerful and beautiful expression. It is exhilarating when we accept who we are and proudly claim that truth to the world. Those identities are important, psychologically and socially, to our well-being. We want to belong to the world, but we also want to be unique, different in some way, from the rest of the world.

This very relationship to time and space, which structures how we interact with the world, also lays the foundation for the emotional pain we all carry around. Our sense of separation means that the world can feel very threatening. If I am separate from you, I can die, and your existence will continue. This is our core fear—the fear of death—and it drives virtually all of our negative emotions in some way, even if the connection seems attenuated or distant. We look at the world and evaluate whether something is going to harm or hurt us, cause us discomfort or support us. We start out evaluating everything in this way, even if it's just a split second. That's why we fear the unknown. It sets off internal alarm bells about what might be, because what might be is something that is a threat to our existence.

Seeing the world in this way is a painful and precarious way to live. But it is what our minds typically do; the ego often feels threatened. As a result, the ego desires constancy in a world where difference, novelty, and change are potential harbingers of danger. Our autonomy, our independence, is also our fragility.

As a result, we typically attempt to strengthen our sense of self by bolstering our identity. When we proclaim an identity, we are also trying to establish a coherent and continuous sense of self, with traits that define us. We declare to the world, "I am

_____." We fill in that blank with characteristics that align us with some people and distinguish us from others—gender, race, sexual orientation, religion, national origin, for example. Some of those categories seem malleable; others seem more permanent. And we have multiple identities, some of which express our associations with others, while others express our preferences and tastes, but not necessarily an affiliation with others.

As part of our effort to defend ourselves, more and more of our self is made to be congruent with and expressive of our identity. Our identities may extend to our hair or clothing, to the ways we carry ourselves and how we speak, to what we think are appropriate emotions, and then sometimes even to the products we buy. In this way, identity can become all-consuming so that every aspect of our lives must connect to this identity. Our identities are presumed to express some inner essence, and thus any quality or aspect that doesn't fit that essence is deemed to be in conflict.[1]

Second, because our egos believe our identities are necessary to our survival, we tend to cling to our identities and defend them constantly. In that way, we are often on alert for where our identity is being undermined or disrespected. It can sometimes feel like we are in a constant state of vigilance, looking to where our identity is ignored so that we are not seen and therefore do not exist. Identities thus function as a defense mechanism against being rendered invisible and unseen, or worse still, subordinated and subjugated. When we defend our identities, we feel that we are defending our existence.

Our conventional model of identity is about opposition to forces of oppression.[2] Identity is the vehicle for recognition and dignity—identities permit us to be seen, valued, and treated equally. All of those are laudable goals, to be sure. But our claims to identity become efforts to gain visibility and resist invisibility.

This is true of the ways that race and sexual orientation came into being. While many still cling to the idea that biological sex is somehow fixed, gender identity has long been seen as much more fluid, as people who are intersex, gender non-binary, and transgender shattered the illusion that gender is a strictly binary proposition. Yet the history of civil rights reminds us that much of the energy we spend in protecting identities arises out of a need to prevent discrimination and opposition to difference. Fear of people whose skin did not resemble their own caused men in the eighteenth century to conjure up a notion of race; fear of sexual desire among same-sex partners generated a taxonomy that produced homosexuality and heterosexuality, along with the criminalization of same-sex desire.

In short, our model of identity is very often tied to conflict over who is deemed valid and belongs, and who is deemed lesser and does not. Indeed, for many people, identity is what prevents them from being invisible, lost, and forgotten, or worse still, punished and killed. Identities, from this perspective, are necessary shields against repression. Without them, we would not be able to resist annihilation, because those who are afraid of difference would then be able to eliminate that difference. In this way, identities, as we currently use them, are primarily defense mechanisms against erasure by another person or group who sees us as a threat, or by a society that would prefer we remain invisible. Identities are necessary to protect us from those who are threatened by difference. That is the touchstone of our identity-based consciousness: I am *this*, and *this* is not *that*. And *that* is a threat to me, so *this* is a better way of being, and *that* should be eradicated.

The fundamental problem is that this effort to define ourselves through our identities is insufficient to the task of understanding who we are or protecting ourselves from threats. Our model of identity is built around protecting against the fear of difference yet does not ultimately eradicate our fear of the other.

Our identities are also partial claims to the fullness of our being. The truth is that we are also spirit—an infinite self or divine being—occupying a human body in this world. That spirit is not limited to these identities. All of us have emotions, desires, expressions, and tastes that exceed the rigid categories in which we often box ourselves. Our identities only capture a part of our totality. Part of ourselves is never captured by our identities, and part of who we are is always changing in small ways. As a result, our sense of who we are, what we are capable of, and how we want to express ourselves is also always changing.

Seekers on a spiritual path will, at one point or another, come to recognize the fluid, almost ghostly, nature of the ego that craves solidity. If we attempt to answer the question of who we are, we may find that any answer we offer slips through our fingers like sand. Many traditions, from Buddhism to psychology, understand that the self is always changing, and from moment to moment, the ego struggles to maintain this sense of a coherent, singular self.

Spiritual wisdom holds that nothing is fixed or unchanging or constant. The only constant is change; impermanence governs our world. As a result, who we are is also in flux. Even if we perceive some aspects of ourselves as not changing—such as gender identity, race, and sexual orientation—we also age, discover new interests, let go of old habits and create new ones. The spiritual path thus asks us to recognize that we are never a coherent, single self, but an ever-morphing constellation of qualities and conditions that can only experience the present moment. Our efforts to define ourselves, to fix the self into a single, coherent subject over time, are ultimately unavailing. Instead of striving for identity, spirituality says that we can embrace a different way of thinking about the self, one that flows from change and difference, rather than striving to be fixed and coherent.

Yet once again, the tendency is somehow that we need to escape ourselves, flee, or leave something entirely behind. A prevailing belief in spiritual communities is that the only path to enlightenment is to have no sense of self. That belief is born in the very idea of returning to our soul, connecting with the divine, realizing that there is no core self. It's like the idea that we'll never feel pain, we'll always be in the bliss of the now, we'll never die because we're eternal souls. We assume that we transcend one set of ideas and find ourselves at a new level of consciousness where the other—the pain of the body, the reality of time, the separation of ourselves into individuals—can be left behind.

The answer that some spiritual traditions offer is that any claim to a self is illusion. That is true, but only partially so. When you embrace the ever-changing nature of the self as a mirage created by the mind, that shift in consciousness comes with its own experience of bliss, peace, and joy as you let go of so much psychic energy bound up in trying to be "me." As I described in previous chapters, I have experienced divine bliss or union in which my sense of self dissolved as kundalini energy moved through my body. I have felt myself feel as though I were nothing but a series of moments, of causes and conditions in Buddhist lingo, where I was just awareness. I have felt myself lose all sense of an "I" and all capacity for language while on ayahuasca. As I described in the last chapter, I have experienced what can be called *samadhi*, where my mind dissolved into light and I felt almost gone. Those experiences are magical and blissful and remarkable for their contrast with our everyday consciousness.

But I have returned to a sense of self, to an "I," had my words restored, felt myself back in my body—and that is a gift too. There's a risk in chasing that bliss, the relief from the baggage of being a human being, of losing that identity and the respite it offers from the existential questions we have about ourselves. For however much our identities may be illusory, we treat them as real and therefore they have real world consequences. We cannot all interact with each other and pretend that we don't have separate selves with some sense of identity.

The spiritual solution to identity does not lie in jettisoning any sense of a self. It does not lie in treating all identity as illusion, just as the solution to the pain of emotion does not lie in numbing yourself or being perpetually positive; or the solution to the limitations of being in a body does not lie in escaping your body; or the solution to our problems with time does not lie in ignoring the past or the future. This is not unlike the claim that only the present moment is real because the other dimensions of time are illusory. Just as there is no way of living without a sense of time, neither can we live without identities. Paradoxically, the fact that they are illusion does not actually undermine their power to shape our lives.

As you may have gathered, the path to liberation never lies in rejecting some part of the equation for another. It lies in embracing the contradiction. We must come to a different understanding of what it means to have an identity, where repression and escapist bliss are not the beginning and final chapters in the story of our lives. Between holding onto identities as shields against dissolution or rejecting identity as pure illusion, we can chart a different course.

FROM SEPARATION TO ONENESS

The path to liberation begins with reframing what we understand by a separate self. Identity, as the ego sees it, is the expression of a mind that believes in separation, that we are separate, autonomous individuals. On a relative, everyday level, this is true. On another level, however, this is false. We are not autonomous, but entirely interdependent. We are like cells of a single organism, working together to create our world. Our lives are never lived in isolation, nor are we that different. Our fundamental needs for material support and emotional well-being—for food, water, shelter, companionship, and love—are shared by all of us.

This is the basic concept of *oneness*. We are interconnected and never truly separate from one another, even if we occupy these physical bodies and exercise free will. We have never been truly isolated. Our lives are enmeshed with the lives of others. We began on this planet dependent on others for our caretaking, and in almost every respect, we remain dependent on others for food, shelter, and medicine. Nor do we seek to live in complete isolation; we are social creatures, seeking connection.

Oneness also recognizes that each of us is spirit in a material body. All of us are divine. Each of us has a direct and inherent connection to God; it is our birthright. Some of us may spend more time fostering that inherent connection, but all of us are capable of awakening at any moment and pursuing a spiritual path. When you see someone, whatever their physical form may be, whatever roles they play in the world, whatever their beliefs are at that moment, they are still divine.

What this means is that oneness recognizes sameness within difference. Oneness doesn't mean the end of difference. All differences—not just the categories we currently recognize and hold onto—are respected. By starting from the premise that we are divine and whole already, we do not need to fear otherness as a threat. This is the fundamental belief that needs to be uprooted and released, which stems from the idea of separation. Instead, the spiritual outlook rooted in oneness regards other people's differences as equally valid expressions of the infinite possibilities that a human form can take. As you awaken and let go of the survivalist mentality that characterizes most of humanity, then others' differences are no longer threatening to you. Nor would you need to engage in the kind of defensive protectionism of your existence, because however you expressed yourself would be seen as a valid expression of your humanity.

Put differently, our task is to hold both identity and divinity, separation and oneness, simultaneously. If we no longer need to protect ourselves with identities as shields because others do not feel threatened by our differences, then we can hold our identities much more lightly, with a greater sense of play and without the constant vigilance for the ways they might be undermined. In this way, oneness is not at all about imposing a model of sameness or homogeneity. It is not some kind of drab totalitarianism in which sameness is imposed, and our lack of identities make us all resemble one another. Such an idea is like assuming that all flowers must be the same because they all are part of nature. We are all nature, and yet we are all different; we are all divine, yet that divinity comes in many forms.

This approach to identity is what flows naturally from the work of accepting emotions, releasing beliefs about oneself, and connecting with the energy of love and compassion at your core. These practices all go hand in hand, lifting you out of fear and into love. The more your consciousness opens and becomes increasingly expansive, the more you regard everyone's expression of their humanity as equally valid. As your heart opens, the walls of your mind no longer seek to defend your identity in the same way. You do not judge someone as better or worse or attach value to the kind of expression they have. You see the identity categories for what they are—constructs of a human consciousness that attempts to separate each individual and render them visible according to certain categories or traits. You see how identities are used to defend and justify those differences, by elevating some and subordinating others, which in turn creates our need to defend ourselves. Once we relinquish this approach, however, we can see our various traits as part of a constantly transforming divine being whose capacity for expression and change is far greater than our limited categories would suggest. Identity becomes a form of creative play, a dynamic experiment of possibility.

The absence of attachment to identity actually gifts us the freedom to express ourselves in new and different ways. We can continue to see each other through the most common categories of identity (i.e., gender, race, sexual orientation, national origin), but we do not need to see them in opposition, as if inhabiting one meant being in conflict with another. We recognize that they are constructs and capable of being changed. Social subordination of one group by another is unnecessary, because our identifications are not rooted in self-preservation from some outside threat. Similarly, the other that produces so much fear in us can also be embraced internally. We need no longer strive for some kind of coherence. Our identities need not eliminate any internal difference. We can be contradictory and incoherent. With a new understanding of identity, we need not suppress our inherent penchant for change.

PRIVILEGE AND RESPONSIBILITY

Releasing our attachment to identity is the challenge that spirituality presents, but we do not all face that task on equal footing. For many, their identities are subject to considerably greater attack. Systemic discrimination based on race, gender, and sexual orientation makes some people's place in this world more precarious. Indeed, for many such groups, their lived experience is one in which identity seems like a critical foothold, something to defend at all costs because their identities have been denigrated, questioned, and threatened.

For each of us to flourish, we must free ourselves from the systemic forms of inequality that are deeply embedded in the fabric of our society. We must all work to undo the oppressive and normative structures around race, gender, sexual orientation, ethnicity, and national origin—all of the ways that we define ourselves that have been built up through cultural stories about the value and meaning of those identities. This is the primary way that inner work helps transform our world, and the work that each of us must take is to release any limiting narratives we tell ourselves based on these categories of identity.

Spirituality asks us to move beyond our current models of identity, to embrace our inherent oneness. What that means is that our differences are no longer how we define and defend our places in the world, because our places in the world shouldn't need definition or defense. But that is not true as a matter of lived experience. The need to champion the rights of and pass laws in defense of certain groups remains a necessary tool to ensure that peoples' lives are protected.

But our awareness of this reality means that privilege begets responsibility. The burden is on the dominant group to let go of their attachment to their identity. White people need to address white privilege, straight people need to address heteronormativity, and men need to address patriarchy. When the dominant group that benefits from the identity structure releases its attachment to that identity, and thus to the benefits of any hierarchy or stratification based on that identity, the need for the minority identity to protect itself, to defend its own identity from attack by the majority, will lessen and ultimately disappear. This is the responsibility that spirituality asks of each of us, so that we might contribute to the creation of a world where oneness is reality.

As a result, our very concept of "identity" would shift away from its protective role. We would approach each other with great curiosity and respect for our "fullness"—all of the characteristics that are part of our psyches and lived history that don't neatly fit into preconceived boxes and labels. All these characteristics would be options reflecting ever-expanding possibilities of what it means to be human. And those differences would be a source of awe, wonder, and curiosity, not fear or disgust.

But what would it mean to say that you are black or white, gay or straight, or male or female? As with all the labels we use to define ourselves, those very categories would shift, evolve, and perhaps even disappear, to be replaced with something else. I would see you and you would see me, in our complexity, as different ways of life taking form, without reducing each of us to a discrete set of categories and without erasing our differences or pretending they didn't shape the course of our lives. In that kind of world, our very existence would be rooted in the belief that our humanity, our right to belong, and our basic goodness are not up for debate or negotiation. Our identities would not serve as bulwarks that guarantee our existence, separate and distinct from each other.

But this is not a call for everyone to jettison their identities or act as if they don't exist. This is why spiritual calls to embrace selflessness or the illusion of identity often fall flat. That's the same kind of naïve thinking that leads people who claim not to perceive race to avoid confronting their privilege or rooting out their conscious and unconscious biases. We can't ignore that our categories of identity, along with their systemic imbalances, exist. They are already a part of our collective consciousness. But they exist because we have created them. Their historical evolution may make them malleable, but that kind of transformation takes time and effort; merely pointing out their constructed nature is not enough to displace them.[3] Rather, consider this a call to hold them more *gently.* Hold them without clinging quite so tightly to them, for yourself and others, because many people still do need the life raft to feel that they belong, and no one's spiritual growth can be rushed. As we progress on the spiritual path, we come to worry less about self-preservation; our fear of difference diminishes. The natural result of that shift in our minds is that our grip on our identities, as the anchor that guarantees our presence here, loosens and softens.

This is the promise of the spiritual path, and why it is incumbent upon us to wake up to our true nature. Until we all see one another as equally worthy manifestations of the divine, with life allowing for novel and new ways of being, our journey is not complete. Where we have privilege, we should deploy it in the service of that awakening. For as we awaken to our true nature, as utterly perfect and divine creations capable of living in unity with the rest of the world, we can regard our identities as a kind of a stepping-stone, a way of claiming our place in the world until we realize that we no longer need to do so. We can then help others to embrace the fundamental truth that we all belong in this realm, not because we claim an identity and demand that others see us as such, but because we are all spirit made flesh. That is the promise of oneness.

YOU ARE MORE THAN YOUR STORY

When you recast your identity as a form of creative play, you now get to answer the question of who you are in a different way. You may, of course, still answer this question with certain characteristics—gender, sex, race, national origin, sexual orientation—or with roles that you play in the lives of others, such as husband or mother—or with roles that you play professionally, such as editor or engineer. You might also describe your personality, situate yourself geographically, or point to your place and time of birth. You might point to qualities you embody. Your perception of these labels may not shift, for when you ask yourself who you are, you realize that there are an infinite number of ways to answer the question.

Hence, you might still be left with the question of who you really are. The question may send you searching for answers. You may soon realize that, like *The Alchemist*, the initial answer to the question is a story: We create a narrative with a beginning and a middle, with different episodes of our life serving as chapters. We speak of being on a journey or a path. We give ourselves the comfort of a trajectory, as if there might be a destination or a destiny that we will eventually reach or fulfill.

It is, above all, a story in which we are the central character. There may be many other central characters, as well as a few villains or a nemesis. We may cultivate a genre in our minds, whether our life is more of a tragedy or a comedy. We define ourselves according to the description we give to the past events of our lives and how they foreshadow what came later or what is still to come. Our self is simply the "I" that writes the story of our identity.

The problem with crafting a story is not that we have one; it's that it always feels incomplete. In this pursuit of self, it never fails to amaze me how much the perception of others seems to matter. For all this inner knowledge, there's still a desire to be recognized by others in the ways that we see ourselves. You might think this is a flaw, a failure that needs to be uprooted. Or you might pause and wonder if this is an expression of our inherent oneness and desire for connection. If the world is our mirror, if what we see is our perception, it seems almost logical to want that mirror to reflect back to us our truest, most authentic expression. How often, then, do we ask ourselves if others really see us for who we are?

We try on new labels almost like garments, only to find over time that they no longer fit because we have grown. We are also always left with a sense of being incomplete, that our fullness is not captured in our public identities. The words we use to describe ourselves leave part of us out, unseen, and invisible to the world. You might add some more words to the mix, but eventually something else will cry out for attention. You'll find that the other words are inadequate, that they've left out some part of you that also clamors for recognition.

It can be exhilarating when you feel seen for who you truly are, or when you find new words for yourself. This is especially true when we embrace a label that once inspired fear or trepidation, such as when you embrace a truth about yourself with the power of a single word. Honoring parts of yourself that you previously hid with shame—declaring your truth to the world without fear of disapproval—is one of the most powerful actions you can take. I recall the power of admitting to myself that I was gay and using that word to describe myself for the first time. Until that moment, I had deluded myself that my desire wasn't really desire but rather a form of identification; in other words, I wanted to *be like* men rather than accept that I *liked* men. Once I embraced the word and shirked off my shame, I felt an incredible sense of freedom to act and express myself in ways that I had refused out of fear.

But even when we "see" each other through labels, we aren't always hitting the mark. When I use a particular label, I rely on my understanding and experience of it, with all of its collective history. But your understanding and experience of that label are different from mine. So even if we use the same word, my use will never fully capture your use of it. In that way, even though we use the same words, we speak different languages.

No matter how many words I might gather to stitch together a self, there are parts of me that live beyond words. In that way, our words always seem inadequate to the task of fulfilling our deep longing to be seen wholly and completely. A gap remains between me and those labels, however much they might be a partial truth. These are, in that regard, competing desires—the desire to be seen and accepted, on the one hand, and on the other, the desire not to be limited by labels that do not capture our full range of being. Beneath our story of identity is a yearning, a sense that there is still some unseen part of us that aches to find expression and be seen.

Rather than see that painful invisibility as a failure of language, we might regard it instead as a source of creativity and wonder. How much else about myself or another was left to discover? What other words might be invented to share the parts of ourselves that seemed beyond words? Can you also see me beyond the words we already know? Knowing that there is always more to see, that our fullness will never be fully captured by labels—that is, at least in part, what fuels intimacy and connection.

From a spiritual perspective, the parts of us that are beyond words reflect the infinite depth of the divine inside of us. If our soul is infinite, that means that we will never be fully known, even to ourselves. We could lament the fact that no amount of words will ever fully capture our wholeness. We could decry the fact that some part of us will always be beyond language. But instead of seeing this as a limitation, we can regard it as an opportunity for creation. We can always continue to explore ourselves and discover new words and ways of talking about who we are. Language then flourishes from that great need to identify the parts of ourselves for which there are no words or for which the words we have no longer quite fit. Instead of feeling dissatisfaction for not being fully seen or known, we can instead cultivate a kind of reverence for the infinite and unknowable aspect of the self. Instead of lamenting this aspect of the human condition, exploring the unknown is the path of discovery: An endless pursuit of what else we might be becomes a play of infinite creativity. This infinite depth of being is what allows us to keep adding new chapters to the story of who we are. Your story is always being rewritten, over and over, in each new moment.

* * *

Whenever I look at pictures of myself as a young baby, I wonder if where I am today was part of a divine blueprint, some path already charted by my soul in concert with the divine, or if who I am today is just one of an infinite number of paths that I could have taken to reach this point. Maybe there is no difference in these two points of view. Nevertheless, sometimes I like to ponder whether there is a multiverse of selves, different versions of me who have taken different paths, made different choices, and have ended up elsewhere, in different careers, in different relationships, with a different perspective on life. Would I like one of these other versions of myself? Would they recognize or like me? Would one of them be jealous of the life I am leading or, on the contrary, would I be jealous of them?

Asking yourself who you are and why you are here opens up a Pandora's box filled with more questions. They are all still part of this existential yearning to know the self. That is what life presents to us in each moment: an opportunity to know ourselves. You are the consciousness that asks these questions, and you are the only one who can answer them. We no longer have to think of identity as something that has to be fixed and defended when we embrace the truth that we are the consciousness that asks to be seen and known, yet defies definition.

We find ourselves moving between the poles of fixture and fluidity, trying on something new, finding it doesn't fit, allowing the world to shape us, and then also exerting our own wills to rewrite our story. Our history is not fixed; the past can be reshaped and molded, but not denied. We neither need to identify ourselves once and for all time, nor refuse the impulse to know ourselves. We must accept this contradiction at the core of our being and live from there. You seek visibility in the world with a mask that doesn't quite fit, yet you can't even claim to fully know what's behind the mask. Accept that you may never fully be yourself, never fully express all that you can be. Embrace the play that comes from having a sense of self, an identity that is never complete, never fixed, and never the totality of who you are. In doing so, you embrace difference, incoherence, and complexity within yourself, which in turn allows you to embrace it in the world. This is the paradox of our claims of identity.

That is ultimately the truth of who we are: portals to infinite dimensions of human life. Identity and the categories we use are way stations, temporary and partial ways of honoring our commonalities, of attempting to take the infinite in us and acknowledge it, make it visible—even if only for a moment. That sense of identity and self is a gift. That it might change or never be fully realized doesn't make it any less of a gift. In fact, it is the wonder and possibility of finding more of yourself, of learning more of who you are, that is life's great mystery. There is immense joy in being able to write and rewrite the story of who we are. Identity is simply the story that you, this divine consciousness, are writing in this very moment. When you ask the question of who you are, it opens you to infinite possibilities. You are light taking countless forms. You cannot be fixed. Why should you be?

RESURRECTION:

EACH MOMENT YOU ARE
A NEW CREATION

⫸

Rewriting my story and playing with the labels that describe myself has not always been a source of joy or creativity. Nor has it always been my choice.

It was the fall of 2010, and I was sitting in the emergency room for the second time that month, overcome with panic. On paper my life looked quite admirable. I had graduated *magna cum laude* from a top law school, and I was clerking on the Court of Appeals, the court just below the Supreme Court of the United States. I had recently been offered a prestigious teaching fellowship at Harvard Law School that would have paved the way to a teaching position as a law professor.

My gut, though, was telling me not to take it. Every morning, I would wake up with knots in my stomach. I wrestled with the decision night and day. I didn't know why, but there was some part of me that knew that I just couldn't accept it. But it was *Harvard Law School*. My gut was screaming at me to let go of this, and eventually I did, but the decision left me a nervous wreck, because never before had my mind and intuition been so at odds. My mentors were aghast, as I had no rational explanation for them. I did not know what I would do next, as the mere thought of the long working hours as an attorney in New

York City sent me into a panic. I became a machine of worry and rumination, churning with anxiety morning and night.

I did not understand at the time that I was going through what is commonly called a "dark night of the soul." It is a form of ego death and resurrection. It is a forced rewriting of your story, where the self evolves under immense pressure without your conscious will. This is a time when your life, which seemed stable and had a solid foundation, turns to quicksand. A long-term relationship ends, you get fired, you get sick, or some combination of these kinds of existential crises takes place, sometimes one after another. You feel like the world isn't a safe place anymore. These moments force you to look within and ask yourself why you're here and what you're doing with your life. Life is asking you to look clearly at how you've been living yours, with the possibility of opening up to a different way of being and a deeper connection with the world.

The dark night of the soul can be a profound, if painful, catalyst for spiritual awakening. It was for me. It was a moment where I had to face some fairly painful truths about myself, wade through the murky waters of my psyche, and eventually recover. Throughout the process, which included dubious attempts to manage my awakening through prescription medication, I thought I was dying. Little did I know that I was being reborn. This is the practice of resurrection, where old identities are shed and new ones created in dramatic fashion.

Resurrection is an essential part of the spiritual path. Yet very often this kind of forced awakening, where parts of you are forced to be shed, can feel like the universe is punishing you or you have failed in some way. Spiritual seekers already on the path can see it as a form of backsliding, some sign that they haven't cleansed enough or kept their "vibration" high enough to avoid calamity. Resurrection reminds you that you are not alone in the creation of your life. Time, in the form of karma, and the demands of your soul, can often drive the direction of your life. You do not always get to choose who you are and where you go. This is the flipside of identity and the crafting of a self over time. Parts of you need to be released, sometimes parts of you that you refuse to relinquish. Your soul knows better. You are imbued with free will, yet the divine will shapes your life in ways that you cannot always anticipate or control. It is through resurrection that we learn that in each moment, we are recreated, with every moment an opportunity to align more closely with our soul.

EGO DEATH AND SOVEREIGNTY

If my dark night of the soul was a moment of ego death and rebirth, it certainly was not my last. The death of the ego does not usually happen in a single instance. I have had countless experiences where parts of myself that no longer served had to perish so that they could be released.

You soon realize as you progress on your spiritual path that you are a quixotic patchwork of ideas, beliefs, memories, and emotions. The person you are today is an amalgam of different versions of yourself that you formed in response to parents, teachers, and other adult figures of authority, as well as friends and siblings. Sometimes, as with the dark night of the soul, the universe and your soul conspire to move you along quickly, even dramatically, to let go of a version of yourself that no longer serves your highest purpose. Your world collapses around you, razed and burnt to the ground, so that out of the ashes you might spring like a phoenix reborn. Transformation is forced and can itself lay a foundation for more pain or trauma when you have no framework for understanding why life is pummeling you. The world can seem cruel—God, a vengeful jester having a laugh at your expense, or you, the person with terrible luck. Your life will change suddenly, but the new you will have to do some inner healing to make sense of the calamity.

Not all resurrections need to be so dramatic and life-altering to be powerful. A very potent resurrection occurred during the third night of an ayahuasca retreat. Under the effects of the plant medicine, I babbled nonstop for hours and hours, sharing all of my secrets, particularly sexual ones, to my fellow travelers. Thankfully, everyone else was on their own psychedelic journey, except for the two facilitators who were there to watch over us. Having been privy to my loud and erotic revelations, the facilitators blushed the next day when the group shared our experiences from the night before. For me, the forced confession, where I spilled the tea in exquisite, salacious detail, was a wonderful exercise in loss of control and loss of self. Mother Nature brought hidden parts of me to light and expelled them because they no longer served me. The same may be said of my kundalini awakening, which happened spontaneously and forced me to relinquish parts of myself that I never consciously sought or desired.

You are here to discover the truth that you resurrect yourself all the time. This is because each moment is a single creation, the present moment, gone in an instant, replaced by the next. In the crucible of the present moment, you have the enormous creative power to declare who you are. Each moment is your creation of the world you experience. In the spiritual realm, this is known as *sovereignty*. It is closely related to, but distinct from, identity. You realize that each and every moment presents an opportunity for death and resurrection, for a new you to be born when you so choose. Each instant of time—the only time that exists for the mind—is a new creation.

This is the power of self-definition. Our sense of identity often takes the form of the question "Who am I?" A better question might be: Who do I *choose* to be in this moment? Your capacity to choose who you are, from moment to moment, is your sovereign capacity to shape your life. You choose now, and in every such moment, how you relate to the past, the present, and the future. Experiences like a dark night of the soul force your transformation, but transformation is available to you in every moment. When you embrace your power in this process, you come to realize that transformation need not be so painful.

Despite our sovereign authority to make choices, we often choose to reclaim ourselves as we have in the past. There is nothing inherently wrong in that process. That is, of course, what we do with identity; we proclaim a sense that will, to some degree, remain constant over time. It's not as if our former selves all need to be jettisoned in the pursuit of some idealized state of enlightenment. It's not as if our current selves are wholly unworthy and must be replaced by some new identity. That is the path of self-immolation, where we do not love any part of ourselves. We deny our inherent worthiness and lovability when we see those parts of ourselves as flaws rather than, as we discussed in Chapter 1, portals to our divinity. Yet all too often, we fall prey to this tendency, and we reclaim again and again our status as victims of circumstance. We bind ourselves to the past, as a kind of straight jacket, so that our thoughts of the future often resemble those of the past. We close ourselves off from possibility and thus from the unknown. In essence, we trap ourselves in a time loop.

CORE BELIEFS

In the face of this time loop, you must recognize your own power, the role of your mind, in creating the reality that you perceive. It is true that you are an amalgam of prior experiences: Concepts you've inherited, even the DNA of your body, is tied to the past. You might be awash in traumatic pain, suffering from prior abuses and betrayals. Your future might look bleak, with few options. At this very moment, though, you have the extraordinary power of claiming your relationship to the world.

The power resides in the words "I am _____" and "I choose _____." How you complete those statements is up to you. You might complete them unconsciously, or painfully, with self-deprecation and self-judgment, or with fear. You are not alone in this. The moment you do, you also have the power to relate differently to that act of self-judgment. This is your conscious power to change at every instance of the now. Everything you experience is your mind's perception and interpretation—including your own tendency to talk negatively about yourself.

We all have parts of ourselves that we want to escape, and we all have parts of ourselves that somehow get hidden because they don't fit our public persona. Holidays like Halloween and Carnival, or cultural phenomena like drag, are perfect examples of our desire to move beyond the identities we fashioned in response to circumstances we did not choose. These are the culturally sanctioned ways we choose to be someone else, if only for a brief period. We know the joy of allowing parts of ourselves to be expressed outside the rigid confines of who we present to the world, and we discover along the way parts we never really knew existed before.

We don't have to wait for culturally sanctioned holidays

or practices to allow ourselves this kind of exploration. This is your innate power: You are divinity in action. Begin with the words you use to talk about yourself. What picture are you painting with them? Every word you use is a form of creation. Your words are *constitutive*—they constitute the reality that you perceive. We saw this process with identity, but our words need not be limited to ourselves. Your words create you *and* your world. What are you creating with the language you use when you speak about yourself? When you speak about the world?

You may be surprised at the language you discover. You may find, if you open yourself to brutal honesty, how poorly you speak of yourself. As you begin to peel back the layers of who you are and why you declare yourself to be a certain way, you come to realize just how much of the present is the past recycled. Older versions of yourself served their function. You can honor them. You are this plethora of older versions, the sediment of past time. With each release, each time you shed a skin, you create more room for the inner light to shine that much brighter. These are the subtleties that you must figure out for yourself as you unwind the patterns, the generational trauma, the emotional burdens you have inherited from your parents and their parents.

Between the everyday choices you make in the moment and the dramatic transformations of the dark night of the soul is the more incremental, and often slow, work of disinterring the older versions of yourself that still persist. It is the work of undoing the beliefs that hold you back and constrict your vision of what's possible. It is the work of unearthing your inner child who still bears so many scars and learned to hide from the world as a way to remain safe. That work takes time, for you soon realize that your power of self-creation, your power to choose your life, does not simply wash away the pain, as if you might will the wound away with a flick of the wrist or a simple declaration that you are now unburdened.

If we are willing to look closely enough at ourselves, we recognize that we are products of our upbringing, and that our parents, for better or worse, imparted to us a series of beliefs about ourselves and the world. As we grew, we experienced emotional pain, and we did not always know how to process it. We built stories and thought patterns around those events to make sense of the pain, to manage it, and to avoid it in the future. Most of our minds are built around risk and pain management. We form beliefs that serve as tools, and so when we feel emotions, it's because our minds have processed something that triggers a reaction rooted in this prior moment in time. These beliefs help us navigate in the world—or so our minds tell us—so that we can manage emotional pain and avoid it.

In that way, you have core beliefs about who you think you are and what will make you happy. You have core desires—what you most seek or want out of life. You have core fears—what you believe will most cause you pain—all of which funnel back to humanity's core fear of death. You have core beliefs about love and how it should be expressed, and what makes one lovable or not. You have core beliefs about right and wrong, good and bad. In other words, the binary structures that make up the mind have, as their underpinning, a set of beliefs that help you assess which side of the binary you're on.

You also have a lifetime of experiences and relationships that have become the soil in which those beliefs have grown. You point to a particular episode, or your relationship to your parents, as evidence that supports those beliefs. Out of this psychic soup forms a personality, which is literally a façade, a mask, a visage that allows you to navigate interpersonal connection.

Much of that is born out of the emotional pain you have experienced throughout life, around which you developed a host of defense mechanisms and beliefs to make sense of the pain. Not all of it, of course, for we are also, fundamentally, love. That is our essence—the impulse to connect, support, and care for each other is also part of who we are.

Your beliefs about yourself drive your impulses and interactions. You may strive for success, to be perfect, to be smart, to be helpful to others, to be independent, to be unique, to change the world through law or politics, to rebel through some kind of counterculture, to be creative and inspirational, to be famous and well-known, to understand the world through philosophy or science. You find that you have values that subtend your impulses: originality and beauty, justice and freedom, commitment and loyalty, truth and wisdom, love and compassion. You may find yourself drawn to those who are passionate, engaged, and outspoken. You may find yourself drawn to others who are tender, vulnerable, and authentic. You may find yourself preferring the company of many or preferring solitude. You may feel at home in quiet, with harmony and serenity being characteristic of the environment you most seek, or you may desire activity, movement, and noise. You may prefer careful deliberation, planning, and cautious action or bold, impetuous, instinctual moves. You may prefer sarcasm and raw humor, or you might be someone who prioritizes being silly. You might like drama or prefer stoicism.

Another pathway to this inner realm is to ask yourself a series of questions related to the chakras: Do I feel safe in this world? What is my relationship to material goods and money? Do I feel connected to others? What are my beliefs about sex? About relationships? About friendships? Do I see myself as creative? Do I feel like I know who I am? Do I feel like the world allows me to be me? Do I feel like I need to conform to gain approval? What would happen if I were truly myself? When I make a mistake, how do I talk about myself? In what ways am I starting to resemble my parents? Do I feel that I am loved? What conditions do I impose on love? What parts of me are not lovable? Can I draw boundaries with others? Can I express myself? What would happen if I shared how I truly felt? Where does my imagination take me? What kind of world would I live in if I could wave a magic wand? Do I trust myself? Do I feel guided? Do I feel like God is watching over me? Do I feel like God is judging me?

It can be daunting to look within at the beliefs we carry around and the stories we've formed that shape our perception of the world. This is the deep work of unraveling the layers of the self.[1] You recreate the past in the present moment *unconsciously*. These patterns and ways of thinking are sticky; they fasten themselves to you like gum on the bottom of a shoe. These are emotional patterns that are deeply embedded in our bodies, in the energy that makes up our auras. Willpower alone cannot uproot them; they are like entities that remain attached to you, triggered at a moment's notice by a careless phrase, a raised voice, the look on someone's face, or someone else's emotional reaction. You might wonder what power you have to wield over the specters of your parents, whose words you imbibed for so long that it now seems impossible to see your way to another version of yourself.

As you meet these parts of yourself from prior moments in time and embrace them, you know that they can be healed and released, but you may find yourself asking a particular incarnation why that version of you still lingers, despite accepting it over and over again. Even when we realize that the story of who we are is one that we get to write, we struggle with how to rewrite the story we've been telling ourselves for so many years. We have to learn to lead our former selves into the cleansing light of our divine love and compassion so that a new self can be born. This is the practice of resurrection in which we put to rest a former self who remains in pain. We've listened and accepted that pain, but another step is often required. We must learn to forgive.

FORGIVENESS IS YOUR SUPERPOWER

Forgiveness is the spiritual virtue that lays the foundation for resurrection. The most famous story of resurrection is, of course, that of the figure of Jesus Christ. The crucifixion of Jesus on the cross now stands as a symbol of a figure who took on the sins of his fellow humans. Jesus's devotion to God was such that despite his physical death, he was resurrected and returned to life. While some might read this as a literal rendition of events, I read it as a parable of one's power to forgive the harms inflicted by others and be reborn as a new self, unburdened by the pain of the past.

The origin story of the Buddha, who sat beneath the bodhi tree and faced all the desires that the demon Mara sent to him, is also a resurrection story. At the end of the encounter with Mara, the Buddha's ego died, and he was reborn again as a new version of himself. No doubt part of the Buddha's enlightenment involved releasing any judgment he might have had towards himself and others for any kind of emotional conflict that occurred prior to his moment of enlightenment. In other words, even if he did not rely on forgiveness in the way that I am describing here, the Buddha saw his prior life, and all the many versions of himself up to that point, in a new light.

One of my most powerful lessons in forgiveness came from

my father. When I was ten years old, my father abruptly left our family. For years, I resented him for leaving. The look on my mother's face holding his letter, tears running down her face, has long been emblazoned in my memory. I knew what the letter said. The day before, while she was at work, my father had pulled me and my two siblings together in the living room to announce that he was asking her for a divorce.

Most of our post-divorce visits were perfunctory trips to fast-food joints where he would buy us a soda and we'd sit and listen to him ramble about getting his master's degree in physics (he was working on light optics of some kind), and his work in electronics (he would eventually work for Panasonic). As you might imagine, my siblings, who were all younger than me, and I did not have much to contribute to the conversation.

When I turned eighteen, he sent my monthly child support check to my mother with a letter informing her that his "obligation" to me was over. I erupted in anger at being treated as an "obligation" to be fulfilled, like a contract. It was the beginning of a deep fracture that we tried to mend but never really did. Despite making efforts to connect during my college years, intimacy never flourished between us, and our relationship faded. Many years later I would learn that my father had died from complications related to diabetes. It took several more years for me to forgive him.

The common-sense understanding of forgiveness is that we release someone from some claim that they did us wrong. Just like "forgiving" a debt, we let go of our grievance to another person. And the way we typically forgive, by saying "I forgive so-and-so," suggests that it's something you do to or for the other person. You're somehow reaching a judgment that calls for benevolence rather than vengeance, and you relinquish any claim or demand for justice.

But the reality is that forgiveness is primarily *for ourselves*. As Mark Nepo writes in *The Book of Awakening*, "What it really comes down to is the clearness of heart to stop defining who I am by those who have hurt me."[2] For me, forgiveness required letting go of the version of myself that identified as a child abandoned by his father. Forgiveness is an act that allows us to release the anger, frustration, pain, sadness, and grief that we carry around in our hearts and that is directed at this other person. The reason we forgive is that carrying around deep anger and resentment is like poison to our souls. Forgiveness is your power to heal yourself and others. It's not just an act where you let go of your pain. It's an act of *liberation* from a moment in time in which you and another person are still imprisoned. You and the other person remain tethered by your feelings. When you forgive, you are freeing yourself and this other person from that emotional strife and baggage.

It's important to say what forgiveness is not: It's not saying that what the person did was justified or right. It's not saying that the person should be allowed to do it again. It's not saying that you have to forget what happened. Forgiveness is, ultimately, an act of love for yourself because it's simply saying that you let go of the anger and despair that this occurred. Forgiveness is also not a way to bypass our feelings. It's okay to feel anger and grief, especially if those feelings are fresh. Feelings and emotions are meant to be experienced fully. It's just that we don't want to live from those places. We don't want to live from our wounds, nurturing them into martyrdom. When you forgive, you are saying that you are a powerful person who can take responsibility for your emotions. Therefore, the event in question will no longer have emotional power over your life.

The true power of forgiveness is that it resets the clock by *rewriting the past*. That doesn't mean the event goes away or that the event didn't happen. It means that you are now creating *a new meaning* for that event, with a new emotional relationship to what transpired. The pain and interpretation you had for that moment in your life, which is what really matters, is what you get to rewrite.

The meaning that you gave that event, the grievance you continue to nurse, is a story. You created a story line to reflect your feelings. That story line is almost always one of pain and victimization and harm by another. What happened emotionally, rather than the plain facts of what occurred, turns on your perception and perspective.

A typical story that requires forgiveness goes something like this: Someone in your life said or did something to you, and you felt a lot of pain around it. What this person did or said caused you harm, and now you hold anger and resentment toward this person. If you haven't forgiven them, you're still telling yourself that same story, and you're still nursing the same grievance. Over time, your feelings may soften, but they can usually be stoked by thinking about what happened.

The task of forgiving is simple in that it requires you to utter two single words: "I forgive." In the world of language, those words are *performative*. Most of what we say is considered *descriptive*—our language attempts to describe the world. Other language is performative, meaning that it does what it says, such as the phrase, "I promise." Such is the case with forgiveness, where the act of uttering the phrase accomplishes the goal.

Yet forgiveness, however simple in theory, is often quite difficult in practice. We may need to make an effort to forgive someone time and again, finding that a flicker of resentment or a pinch of anger occurs when we reflect on our conflict with them. You haven't forgiven; you've only momentarily forgotten.

The practice must be undertaken until the resentment finally lifts and the emotional reflex dissipates. Then, when you think of this person or event, you can regard it with a sense of balance and understanding, not reactivity.

Forgiveness isn't about denying the past or burying one's memories beneath a façade of reconciliation. Burial of one's pain will only later result in its return in some other, often more ghastly form. Instead, forgiveness requires you to reconfigure the roles each of you played in the story you've been telling yourself. It starts by recognizing a fundamental truth—and many people recoil when they first hear it—but you need to listen closely: The reason this person said or did something to hurt you is because it had *meaning for you*. You *believed* that what they did or said actually expressed something true about you.

You have to accept that you've created this meaning because that's what the wounded part of you can't give up. The wounded part of you was hurt by this meaning, what this story said about you, and the emotions the story brought with it. The way to unwind that meaning is to recognize that it's not necessarily true. Instead, go in search of the story that identifies the wound from which your perpetrator acted. To borrow from Piero Ferrucci in *The Power of Kindness*, "[W]e will be able to forgive if we can place ourselves in another's shoes; if we are less concerned with judgment, and more with understanding."[3]

Understanding my father's pain is what allowed me to forgive him. While I still carried around the resentment of his abandonment, my ten-year-old self had internalized the belief that there was something wrong with me. My only solution— the only hope of getting his attention and, by extension, his love—was to be smart, the kind of person who could talk about the kind of smart things my father liked to discuss.

When I learned my father had died, I was reconnected with his sister, my aunt, whom I had cherished as a kid. We reunited in person, and I began to learn about my father's life during the previous twenty years when we had been estranged. What I learned inspired great sympathy. I learned that his father (my grandfather) had belittled him ceaselessly, criticizing his intellect and making my father profoundly insecure. His solution was to become very smart—to try to win his father's affection.

The pattern had replicated itself with me, except that we ended up not being a part of each other's lives—his wound begat my wound. But when I understood what he had gone through, and how he had spent his life trying to prove that he was smarter than the next guy, and how it had embittered him, I finally understood that my father didn't know how to love any differently. The afternoons in fast-food joints when he prattled about optics and electronics reflected his language of love, and as boring as it was to me, it was the only way he knew how to express kindness, affection, attention, and care.

In that way, I was able to rewrite the story: I forgave him because my story wasn't the story of a young boy whose father didn't love him and spent every other Saturday narcissistically talking about himself. No, my story was the story of a father whose only language of love was science and math, and who spent his time talking about science and math with his children. This is the power of forgiveness: It allows you to create a new story of empowerment and jettison the old one that made you a victim. As David Whyte puts it, forgiveness means that "we allow ourselves to be gifted by a story larger than the story that first hurt us and left us bereft."[4]

And that's what you realize when you genuinely forgive: The story you told was about the emotional impact on *you*. But the real story is the other person's wound. That's not to invalidate your feelings. Yes, you felt pain—I did. It was painful to feel like my dad didn't love me. But that pain was not the truth—it was the pain of my story about what happened. The true story was that my father didn't know how to love me in a way that allowed me to recognize his affection as love. That was his limitation.

This is the long and often bumpy road to forgiveness. You won't always know what the other person's wound is, but you can begin by recognizing that most often, you need to let go of the part of you that felt, or maybe still feels, wounded, and find a new story, a new meaning to that event. In that way, you can feel compassion for someone's deep pain and how they never healed it, which caused them to act out and behave unskillfully. When you can tap into that compassion, you give yourself the capacity to forgive them for their actions, and forgive yourself for holding onto the story of your pain for so long.

THE POWER OF APOLOGY

One of the reasons that we hold onto our stories is because we are waiting for an apology. When another person hurts us and we blame them for our pain, we often expect them to repair the situation by issuing an apology. When we do so, we conflate apology with forgiveness, expecting the first to allow for the second.

I believe wholeheartedly in the power of apology. Reaching out to someone and apologizing for your behavior is one of the most potent ways of rewriting the story that you have crafted in your head. All too often conflicts harden into entrenched opposition, with each person regarding the other as an adversary. Over time, the breach in the relationship deepens, forming something like a scar whose tissue is no longer capable of being mended. We stew in our mental juices, reliving the conflict for anyone who will listen, or we see every subsequent conversation as another salvo in a never-ending battle. There is no room for forgiveness when the other becomes a foe who must be vanquished.

Yet it is not weakness to acknowledge where your words and actions, driven by your emotional responses, have contributed to the present divide in a relationship. It takes enormous strength and vulnerability to take responsibility and offer an apology. Doing so can immediately allow the other person to relax, drop their verbal weapons, and climb out of their emotional bunker. More often than not, a sincere and heartfelt apology enables a renewed form of communication that would have seemed impossible previously.

Apology can be particularly hard when you are attached to always being right. Those of us in that camp might view apology as a sign of weakness. For years, I felt much more inclined to hold my ground. Unwilling to relent, I held fast to the righteousness of my status as a victim. Instead, over time, I have come to appreciate just how much every interaction is the creation of two minds coming together. Each person contributes to the conflict in some way. That does not mean that there is no room to recognize that you may be more responsible than the other for what transpired, when the other person simply served as a mirror to trigger an old pattern in you. The awareness of yourself and maturity to see yourself clearly should enable you to acknowledge how you've behaved. Embracing the power of apology has often led to the rapprochement that we often seek in attempting this kind of reconnection. Apology can pave the way for the other to forgive more freely. Once your apology has given them a new understanding of what transpired between you, they can release their story of victimhood.

From there, apology and forgiveness can lead to reconciliation. But not always. We sometimes expect that forgiveness will automatically lead to some kind of reconciliation. It can, of course, mend a broken relationship. But forgiveness is not, at its core, about reconciliation or reconnection. Forgiveness is fundamentally about you healing the part of you that is wounded by what occurred—some word or action by the other person that harmed you, and by extension, the relationship.

When we conflate apology with forgiveness, by giving one to get the other, we set ourselves up for disappointment. Sometimes the other person is not available, as was the case with my father. Sometimes the other person cannot bear to let go of their pain to listen to your apology. The pain is too great, and they remain attached to the position of moral authority that being a victim affords. In other words, forgiveness does not produce the apology we were seeking. Occasionally, when this happens, we lament that we've apologized, and the other person continues to bear a grudge. It means that we still have not forgiven ourselves or the other person. We used apology to obtain a reconciliation that we were denied, and now the breach is revived. We are likely to be disappointed when we are unwilling to forgive and instead wait for the other person to apologize. When we wait for the other person to acknowledge our pain because we think that's how healing should happen, we've relinquished the power of our healing to the other person. You recover your sovereign power to choose who you are and what your life means when you choose to forgive, and in so doing, heal a wounded part of you. After all, the pain was never telling you the truth of who you are.

* * *

Forgiveness is a critical step in the practice of resurrection. We allow a certain version of our story to die, and a new version of us is born. In this way, forgiveness is a form of time travel. While we cannot undo the events of the past, we certainly can reinterpret them and how they have shaped our lives. When we walk down memory lane to revisit a prior painful event, we often revive the emotions that we experienced at the time. We also revive the story, our interpretation, of what happened back then. If you recount some prior trauma to someone else, you may feel yourself flooded with the feelings you experienced then, as if you were experiencing this event again in the present moment. Our memory is this intricate tapestry of thoughts, beliefs, and emotions.

When you forgive, you travel back in time to the memory of your younger self. Rather than eliminating the events in question, you choose a new story. You reinterpret those events, contextualizing them in the broader narrative of your life, thus rewriting the meaning of that event from the perspective of the current self. In so doing, you also can see how the emotions that were tied to that story can shift and release. The younger self, the self who is the lead figure in the memory, stops suffering from whatever painful story he or she had derived from the original experience. You now live a much freer existence, seeing that past moment from the vantage point of wisdom and experience. Our younger self, who we thought was so fixed in time, locked in the prison of the past, is free. The future has shaped the past and has now rewritten the present moment. We release ourselves from the time loop of our pain.

When we lead older versions of ourselves that no longer serve us into the light of our compassion, we recreate ourselves anew. Much of the spiritual path involves allowing parts of yourself that no longer serve you to fade and die. It is sometimes, as this experience was for me, painful and harrowing, but it need not always be. With practice, you can see each and every moment as an opportunity to practice resurrection. Being reborn is something we do all the time.

Freeing ourselves from the repetition of the past enables us to open more freely to the future, to unseen possibilities. We allow ourselves to experience that which we have previously denied ourselves, and to express parts of ourselves that we have kept hidden from view. In so doing, we embrace transformation, not as a singular and often disruptive event, but as the baseline for our lives. Each moment percolates with the power to choose who we will be.

You can be your full self from moment to moment without feeling the need to label yourself or to conform to what others expect of or know about you. You are not beholden to the image you've crafted for the world to consume. You allow yourself to flow into dynamic coordination with your soul in the forms that it wants you to experience and express. You honor the self that changes through time, over time, and is both mortal and immortal, subject to labels and definition but also ineffable and beyond language. You are human, in a body, with a name and a history, yet you are also divine, living spirit, beyond names and beyond history. We open more fully to our divine side the more we reconcile our past by forgiving the moments where we forgot or never believed in our divinity.

The power of resurrection also recognizes, however, that our prior selves do not always want to pass gently into the night. Hence, we sometimes experience a dark night of the soul, where the death of one identity and the rebirth of a new self are forced upon us. Parts of our lives are taken away so that we might experience something new. In my case, I had to release my attachment to an older view of the world and of myself that

had limited me. I became a lawyer while also undergoing a profound spiritual transformation. All of this happened simultaneously, as I let go of my old plans for a life in legal academia.
Instead, I was carried on a journey I could never have anticipated, the discovery of parts of myself that I otherwise would
never have known, had I fulfilled the dream I had chosen for
myself.

In that way, the part of us that knows more—our soul or
higher self—taught me how to allow myself to evolve ever more
gently. We do not always need a dark night of the soul, or even
pain, to learn to grow. Instead, we can embrace our capacity to die and be reborn with ease. Resurrection can become
a source of joy, a regular part of your life. Future transitions,
such as leaving my legal job to work as a writer and spiritual
guide, became much simpler. Nevertheless, at a certain point
I had to look back at that time of forced awakening to see how
hard-headed I had been, how unwilling I had been to let go of a
certain version of myself. I then recognized that I also had to let
go of the part of me that still judged my prior self for making it
so hard, for not understanding what I was experiencing at the
time. My present self had the benefit of hindsight; my prior self
had no idea why the world was falling down around him. In the
end, I did what all resurrection requires: I forgave myself.

CONNECTION:
YOU ARE A TIME TRAVELER

FORGIVENESS REQUIRES THAT we understand that the other person's wound has contributed to our pain, yet it also reminds us that we often know very little about the pain that others carry around in them. That is the crux of the plot in *The Time Traveler's Wife*. In that story (both a film and a book), a husband and wife, Henry and Claire, face an existential problem: The husband is a time traveler, but he has no control over when he travels or for how long. One moment he's there, and the next, his clothes are lying in a pile on the floor. He moves forward and backward in time, showing up at different points in Claire's life. Each time Henry shows up, he's a slightly different Henry, from a different time.

As a parable, the film captures the unique conundrum of time in our relationships. For while we don't leap forward or backward in time, we are, in fact, travelers in each other's worlds. We pop in and out of each other's lives, with many moments in between where we are not in each other's orbit. Each of us experiences time in our own way. My sense of time is not your sense of time; we travel back and forth, intersecting each other's timelines.

This relationship to time is actually quite extraordinary

when you think about it. When we meet people for the first time, we often ask them to situate themselves in time by telling us where they are from or what they do for a living; we ask for a story. Yet when we reconnect with a friend or even our spouse or children at the end of the day, we do the same by asking them to recount how they spent their day. We ask each other to fill in the gaps, from the last time we saw them to the present moment. In this way, we are always strangers to each other, living large pockets of our lives without knowing exactly what the other has been doing, saying, thinking, or feeling. It is out of that lack of knowledge about the other that our conflicts arise. Intimacy and knowledge are built around our capacity to share time—either through stories about our life or by aligning our timelines so that we share time together.

Yet the conundrum posed by time is that no matter what we do, we are always separate from each other in time. This might seem to run counter to the principle of oneness, the fact that we are interdependent and share the same divine spirit. In fact, it is that oneness of spirit that propels us to bridge our separation and connect. We all desire to connect with others, to find people that can share common interests, who love and accept us, and with whom we can build relationships, families, and communities. We seek to embody our innate oneness, moving past our separation while still honoring our autonomy. At the same time, our pain and suffering are indelibly tied to other people. We have all faced rejection, abandonment, or abuse. We find ourselves constantly navigating conflict and disagreement with others. No matter how much we seek to connect, there is never a relationship where some misunderstanding, some moment of rupture, however small, does not arise. Our connections are always tested. Relationships end, couples divorce, families fight, and coworkers squabble and gossip. We fall out of oneness and back into separation, emotionally and in time.

What insight does spirituality offer us for navigating our connections with others? All too often we regurgitate something of a platitude about loving everybody, but it's an intellectual gambit designed to mask our fears, insecurities, and pain. The exhortation to love everybody begs the question of how that is possible and what it means to love. Our desire for connection requires us to accept the conundrum that, even though we are all spirit, we are also ultimately strangers to each other, living in separate dimensions of time.

As we have seen already, the path of spiritual mastery requires that we accept two mutually exclusive truths. The same is true for relationships: First, everyone we encounter is a mirror, reflecting our mind's perceptions and our requirements for loving another person. Second, everyone we encounter is a stranger whose life is mostly unknown and will never be known to us. The path to connection is not, paradoxically, to escape these truths, but to embrace their contradiction and hold them simultaneously. Taken together, they show us how to release the limits that we place on love and on the unknown, which turn out to be the same.

FAMILY MATTERS

In the television show *Unbreakable Kimmy Schmidt*, the lead character, Kimmy, goes to a therapist played by the inimitable Tina Fey, who deals with her own trauma by getting drunk every night. When Kimmy runs into Fey at a mall, the therapist, sloshing about with a spiked Slurpee, confesses, "It's always the parents, Kimmy." Most therapists would likely agree, even if individual cases are always more complex. So, too, have I discovered the same in my intuitive work, where I find that most people are harboring painful patterns learned from their parents.

Many spiritual seekers go in search of wisdom and intuitive advice when facing issues arising from how a parent has failed to express love, such as when a parent abandoned or belittled them. One of the most harrowing feelings I have encountered as an intuitive was working with someone whose mother absolutely did not want to give birth to her; the feeling of pain and loss from that sense of not being loved was overwhelming to me. That loss of love, in turn, had shaped much of this person's relationship to life—her ability to connect to others, to the kind of career she chose, and how she related to life and the ability to connect to the divine inside.

Hence, the work of healing how we connect with and love others almost always begins with our parents or early caretakers. So very often at least one of them occupies an outsize role in our psychic lives; it is from them we learn our first models for connection. Often, but not always, that figure is our mother. We began our physical lives in oneness with our mother, and it is through her that we often learn connection and disconnection. As I have been repeatedly reminded by my spirit guides and plant medicine, our mothers are our birth portal, and we must honor them as much as we can, even when they may also be enormous sources of pain for us. For many of us, but certainly not all of us, mothers are our first major connection, the source of nourishment and comfort.[1] It is a common spiritual joke that we are all enlightened until our mothers show up. We learn early on from them that love can often come with requirements, or takes certain forms, and that love must be given and received in certain ways.

This has certainly been true for me. Early in life, I formed a belief that my mother had not wanted to give birth to me. She had me when she was nineteen, and my entrance into the world ended a budding career in dance, one of her great loves. I believed that my arrival had derailed my mother's career plans and that she resented me for it. The belief played a tremendous role in the sense that I did not belong here and couldn't be accepted by others. When I confessed this to her many years later, she broke into tears because I had taken the courageous step of broaching something that no mother ever wants to confess. It was not that she did not want me, but that she was profoundly worried as a young mother about whether she was up to the task of taking care of me. As a young child, I had felt this unease in her and interpreted it in terms of an absence of love. Many of us carry around vast numbers of misinterpretations that often leave deep psychic scars.

Our fathers, too, often play a critical role in shaping our emotional lives, but the father is often far more symbolic of separation. As a paradigm, fathers teach us about rules and separation. We often learn what emotions are appropriate from our fathers; most boys learn early on that most emotions are to be hidden. From my experience, in life and as an intuitive, fathers, if they are part of our lives, very often represent what it means to deal with emotional absence and a sense of disconnection. By way of example, one of my clients showed up and asked to talk about her sister and husband, and I immediately knew that nothing we talked about relating to them would be what she needed to discuss. I knew, intuitively, that it had everything to do with her father. I asked her to tell me about him, and she stopped and started to tear up. Her father had committed suicide when she was a child, and his death had instilled in her a deep sense of abandonment. She had never worked through it or really disclosed it to many people. As I am not a therapist, I didn't do that deep work with her, but she turned to counseling and later shared with me that she had returned to her home country to make peace with her father. Our encounter was the starting point of a very intense episode of healing for her.

I am painting these relationships with broad brushstrokes. It matters little whether your parents conform to these rough caricatures. In one way or another, we have all felt the sting of reproach, disappointment, and abandonment—some way that the love we felt from our parents was no longer pure or unconditional. Culturally and socially, we extol to almost mythic proportions love without requirements or conditions. Even if they were our first caregivers who did their best, they were also products of our collective consciousness, with their own patterns, pain, and beliefs about life. They had lots of thoughts and ideas about us and what we meant for their lives. So much of this information gets passed on, sometimes unconsciously, to us. For no matter how much our parents loved us, there was always going to be some moment of disappointment or dissatisfaction when you did not get what you wanted, or a rule was imposed, or your mother or father did or said something that felt deflating, dismissive, or hurtful.

In one way or another, through their presence or absence, our relationship with our parents establishes the parameters that we will replicate time and again in our other relationships. We learn from them the conditions for giving and receiving love, and the ways that such love may be expressed. We must look inward at how we think of love and the desire for connection, whether we privilege romantic love or friendship. Each of us has a taxonomy of love, with our own definitions of what that means for partners, lovers, family, or friends. We have an idea of what it means to put someone in one category or another.

We have to look at the rules we impose for giving and receiving love. This is our personal story about love, often infused with but also distinct from the many cultural stories we hear and receive about love.

The ways we give and receive love—the terms we use, the conditions we attach—are sometimes called love languages. They are not necessarily bad and do not always need to be jettisoned; sometimes they simply need to be expanded. The problem is that they very often deprive us of other avenues of love by closing them off to us. We speak one version of love, not realizing that there are so many other ways to give and receive it. For example, one story that you might tell yourself is that romantic love is the highest form of love, and in telling yourself this story, you might believe that there is a single person out there for you—a soul mate, a twin flame—and if you don't find this person, you're failing at love. Or, you find that person and refuse to see other possibilities for receiving love.

To heal this crucible of connection out of which we forge the rest of our relationships, we must forgive our parents. In particular, we must forgive them for the limits on love that we have inherited, so that the ways we connect to others no longer resembles the way our parents relate to each other, to us, and to other people in the world. We do this for our relationships and our children, so that we do not pass along these patterns as a cycle of generational karma. The work begins by reflecting deeply on those sources of pain—the childhood memories, the moments of misunderstanding—to understand the stories that we tell about ourselves and out of which we developed our language of love. It is important to touch this pain gingerly, with great sensitivity, for it is all too easy to plunge into the deep waters of our resentment toward our parents and find ourselves gasping for air.

Forgiveness, as we have seen, can simply begin with the words "I forgive you," and holding the intention to release. Prayer is also highly effective, because it allows you to turn over the task to the divine, by simply asking the divine to help you forgive your parents. There are countless forgiveness practices, but I might suggest you start by writing a letter to your mother or father from the perspective of your younger self, allowing the full extent of your feelings to spill out onto your computer screen. If you have a lovingkindness practice where you offer wishes of safety and well-being to others, incorporate your parents into this practice.[2]

When we do this work of forgiving our parents, we might stumble upon a truth that is as startling as it is obvious: We know so little of our parents and what their own experiences taught them about love and connection.[3] Despite having so much of our lives intertwined with them, they are ultimately quite mysterious to us. Their lives are vast compared to the amount of time we've occupied them. In most cases, at least two decades of their lives went by before we arrived. We also don't know what painful episodes they've endured unless they've opened up to us. That was the case with my biological father, as I discussed in the previous chapter. It took my understanding of what he had endured to be able to truly forgive him for my inherited pattern.

TALKING TO GHOSTS IN MIRRORS

The truth that we know so little about our parents is also true of everyone else. We are all strangers to each other. We cannot avoid this truth, however much we'd like to. So much of another's life is never available to us, and our lives are not available to them. You might spend lots of time with other people; in fact, the majority of your waking hours are likely spent with others. But the time you spend in your head, in your mind, far outpaces the time you spend in conversation or even in the presence of others. You experience countless moments of time alone, in thought, in the moments between speech and listening. We are each of us bends in the fabric of space and time, each living out our own experience of the world.[4] What this means is that you are not quite the same person as you were when you last interacted with someone else, and that is true of the other person, whoever they may be. We are like the universe itself, a vastness that is always expanding. We have each recreated ourselves, perhaps in only marginally important ways, again and again during our absence from each other. We become time travelers in each other's lives.

The tragic consequence of this existential conundrum is that when we do connect, we so rarely meet in the present moment, just as we are. How can I possibly know fully the person who is speaking to me right now? It's true that very little might have changed on the surface, but you are each now interacting with your perception of the other, largely based on memory. You see each other, as we must, through the eyes of the past, even if that past was only but a moment ago. The longer the time between interactions, the more that we find ourselves struggling to reconcile our memory with the person presently before us. It might seem like a sad and poignant truth that even as we get to know each other, we inevitably grow further and further apart from each other, for who we are grows deeper and faster than we can share with others.

To honor that vastness in each other is to honor our inherent divinity. We honor that divinity when we do not bind the other person to our memories and preexisting concepts of who this person must be, how they must feel, and what they must think or believe. This is hardest to do with the people closest to us, for we often develop a clear sense of who they are and rarely leave them with room for change. Instead, it is our task to remember them as they were—years, months, or even just moments ago—and yet hold our memories and images lightly so that we might, at the same time, bear witness to the new person who stands before us, a person who might resemble in so many ways the person we already know but who in other respects is also a stranger.

That is not meant to invite distance or a sense of estrangement. On the contrary, to the extent that it is an unavoidable truth that each of us is so rich in memory and imagination that we'll never fully know each other, we can relate to each other with a sense of wonder and awe. Can I see you now, in the present, in a way that permits your fullness to share itself with me? Can I not foist my memory and perception onto you, imposing expectations of what you might be like, so that I can say to myself that I already know you and what you're going to say or do? The fact that we are strangers means there is always more to know and learn about the other.

Recall the topic of time we discussed in Chapter 3. We do not see the present but our past perceptions. We limit each other with our perceptions. Rather than open myself to the possibility that you might have some new quality, talent, or opinion to share with me, I build a relationship with what I already know. Our connections can sometimes end up being founded on two ghostly mirages, each of us conjuring up an old and outdated version of the other. But we can become aware of this tendency and work to release our perceptions. Instead, when we can approach each other in the present, with fresh eyes, we open ourselves up to a much richer set of possibilities.

We embrace the paradox that we see each other as old friends and complete strangers all at once.

The risk is that we might find something in the other we don't like, that the connection will founder and the relationship will end. But this is also the path to unconditional love, to open ourselves to the love of the stranger in all of us. Isn't one of our great fears that we will share some side of ourselves, and someone else whom we love will reject us? We fear that our vulnerability will trigger some condition of their love, and we'll feel the pain of their withdrawal. The path of unconditional love, then, is not loving that which we know, but loving that which we do not know, so that the other might feel permission to share more of themselves.

One of my closest friends and I discovered a mutual love of a certain composer of cinematic scores some two decades into our relationship. For no particular reason, we simply never thought that the other person might share this interest; our friendship had been built up around certain topics and not others. It never occurred to either of us to broach this topic until happenstance led one of us to remark on it. Yet, in revealing this side of ourselves, a new dimension to the relationship was formed.

To create a true connection, we must be willing to risk losing one by allowing more of ourselves to be seen and shared. This is the joy of vulnerability. We hold tight to a certain view of ourselves and others, of what that relationship can handle, only to then put a stranglehold on possibility. We anticipate rejection and decide that there is only so much intimacy that we can have. Many of us have guarded hearts; we carry within us the scars of betrayal and rejection. That is the energy we carry, acting as a shield to prevent pain, but also keeping people at arm's length, and thus keeping love and intimacy at bay. It takes effort to keep the heart open and vulnerable when it wants to clench tightly.

Yet intimacy cannot be forced. We can go too far in the opposite direction in forcing intimacy. Intimacy blooms with patience and care, each person tending to their own borders and boundaries. We honor the divine in each other, and learn to connect unconditionally, by slowly developing the space where we can share our shadows. We thus court each other's intimacy by neither imprisoning the other in a version of themselves from the past nor forcing revelation before they are ready, but instead being open to the possibility of what might be shared. We must be willing to see the edges of our intimacy as the border where we monitor and surveil our sense of protection and to work with that fear so that we might create deeper relationships. We invite the other by taking that leap of faith and bringing our fullest possible presence to them. We allow our divinity to come through by sharing our heart and the unknown in us.

Ask yourself what aspects of your life you are willing to discuss or share with another person. Again, this is not a call to shed any and all inhibitions about sharing parts of yourself with another person, as if confession and exposure were the only modes of engagement. But by asking this question, you can begin to see how in your relationships you guard against intimacy, how you decide that some topics are acceptable and some are off limits, even in close relationships. Notice where, even in the company of those with whom you feel safe to share, you keep certain parts of yourself hidden. There is nothing inherently wrong in this, except that you may be operating out of shame or fear of disapproval.

You also might be forging new bonds in an old crucible that no longer reflects who you truly are. I have found time and again that when I present myself as a lawyer, people perceive me in a certain way, and if I later reveal myself as a writer and an intuitive, an entirely different connection is formed. It has taken me many years to develop the self-love necessary to share myself freely and authentically instead of wrapping myself in a garment of words designed to be more accessible. In that way, I have often missed opportunities for connection based on an old story that my true self was not acceptable. When we show up as our authentic selves, not trying to present a more easily digestible image, we give permission to others to do the same.

LETTING GO OF UTILITY

One reason that we do not share ourselves easily with strangers is that we fear being used or manipulated. It's true that some may harbor ill will and bad intentions for us. As we get to know someone, we may still harbor the fear that we do not matter but only serve as a tool in the other person's life, and as such, we may be discarded when that other person deems us no longer useful.

We must learn to release this habit in ourselves. As we learn to honor the awe and mystery of another person, we also let go of our expectations for the role the other will serve in our lives. It is a humbling state to see the other as a gift whose purpose will be revealed over time. Others serve as our mirror, reflecting back to us the ways in which we place conditions on love and connection and judge people when they don't satisfy those conditions. For when we meet another, we see each other through our prior perceptions in what might amount to a carnival house of mirrors. This is what is meant by cocreation. You meet me, and you perceive me through your consciousness and all of its concepts and experiences, and I do the same with you.

One of the most common predilections that humans share is the tendency to see people not as sources of wonder and mystery but in a utilitarian manner. The world we live in does not normally teach us to see each person as a poem, a song, or a flower. Rather, we learn very early on to treat another person as a tool, a device, or a bridge to someone else. Love and connection become transactional, with each person acting to obtain something from the other. We stop seeing people as divine creations with full emotional lives when we ask ourselves what this person can do for us. If they do not seem to offer a particular contribution and we lower our opinion of them, we have lost sight of their divinity.

We even do this in our most intimate relationships; an underlying current of utility can insert itself when we think about the emotional benefits that someone we love and adore offers us. It is the path of mastery to love this person in this very moment for the gift of their affection and presence without attaching any kind of transactional aspect to it. If you look closely at even your most cherished relationships, or the most important ones, like a spouse, you can often still find an undercurrent of utility and transaction in them.

THE ART OF REPAIR

Inevitably, all relationships experience disconnection and rupture. It takes strength to share your hurt with another in hopes of repairing the damage and mending the tear in the relationship. You can forgive and heal your pain, but that does not mean that the relationship itself is automatically renewed. Both parties to the relationship must be willing to face the other, to listen and not put up walls of defense, to share their hurt rather than casting stones of blame. This is the art of repair. It requires that we listen with generosity, without anticipating the moment when it is our turn to speak such that our attention is already on what we will say. When we do that, we are impatient and barely paying attention to what the other has to say.

Fostering the willingness to repair requires us to let go of our own pain. Whenever I have felt angry or dismissive of someone, and I have the presence of mind to pause, I ask myself what it would be like to learn that this person had died. Whenever I contemplate this person's absence, knowing that we would never cross paths again, I almost always soften in the moment; my heart tenderizes, and I regain this center that I know is true, beneath the emotional tapestry that I've been weaving with my thoughts. It makes me want to reach out and resolve our conflicts.

Not all relationships will go through repair, however. Some people are not conscious enough, nor have they developed the emotional capacity to feel their pain and listen to yours so that you might both heal through a thoughtful exchange of feelings. That too has been a hard lesson for me, learning to let go of the possibility that a relationship could be repaired when the other party seems unwilling. Those situations are the ones that have often made my heart want to close and barricade itself. When it does, I try to remember that keeping my heart open does not require me to treat the other person as if there were no conflict. It does not mean that I turn the page and pretend that whatever pain they've inflicted never happened. It does mean that I don't have to maintain the same kind of relationship I had before.

Even if the other person is unwilling to repair our connection, I don't need to foster resentment. I don't need to nurse the grievance. I have to accept this person's wounds and capacity for repair and reconnection. That might mean that I continue to love them from a distance. It might mean I accept that this is their path, and the time that we had together has, at least for the moment, come to an end. It might mean remembering that their value in this world is not contingent on remaining connected with me, nor is mine dependent on whether they value me enough to attempt to repair our connection. That is the art of loving while letting go.

Most importantly, we cannot let any resentment about the relationship lead us to use our power of language to speak ill of others and gossip about them. If we speak about others in a way that does not honor their divinity, we engage in a form of blasphemy. We often gossip about others when we've had a conflict with them, and rather than resolving it, we talk about them to others so they'll agree that we were unjustly wronged. We bear a responsibility to use our words carefully when speaking about others, for our words carry immense power to shape perception and thereby create a story that others will consume as truth. This is why the Buddhists emphasize as one of the eight precepts the concept of "right speech." Asking yourself whether what you are about to say about another person is true, kind, and necessary is a good way of reminding yourself that what you share about another person reflects your divine powers of creation.

AFTER AWAKENING

Connections after a spiritual awakening can be tricky. When we begin to see the world differently, it is easy to want others to experience the kind of liberation we've experienced. Sometimes that path involves sharing and realizing that your current friends no longer understand you. But each of us is on our own path, and we cannot be impatient and force another to open, just as nature does not force a flower to bloom before it is ready. We can be open to the possibility that the person next to us will awaken in the next moment, but we cannot try to force that future to arrive before it is ready. Instead, we must allow that person to move in and out of alignment with our lives, honoring who we are now as we honor who they are now. That may mean that people you once knew no longer feel the same connection and may fade out of your life. But it might mean that parts of you that you wouldn't normally share are now available to be seen by the other person.

More often than not, I see spiritual seekers, upon awakening to their true nature and exploring spirituality with zeal, suddenly proclaim that they no longer feel connected to their friends and family and go in search of another community. I understand that impulse. We can feel an intense pressure to separate from those we knew before our awakening because our awakening starts to impose demands on how others should behave. We feel constrained by the former relationship. We're sometimes judged for the new choices we are making. We can draw boundaries, ask to be treated differently and in ways that no longer cause us harm, and we can refrain from activities that no longer inspire us.

But we neither have to demand that others change to conform to our views nor presume that others will reject or abandon us. Countless times I have learned the joy of sharing my spiritual side with others who don't share the same views and yet find that we still have a very strong bond. It can be a wonderful gift to connect with others who are on a similar path, where you don't face the same suspicion or judgment, and do not always have to face internal shame for your choices. But we must be vigilant not to create a new set of criteria or conditions for connecting with and loving another person. We end up replicating our old parameters if we decide that only those who are spiritually awake are worthy of our time and attention.

The challenge is to meet each person as an emissary of the divine. How do we react to the person to whom we have no connection whatsoever? How do we treat the true stranger? We meet them as equally divine as we meet our closest friends and loved ones. The famous quotation by Ram Dass that we are all God in drag, or the pop song that asks, "What if God were one of us?" both offer the same wisdom—namely, to see each other as the divine made flesh.

That does not mean that you subordinate your needs to everyone else, or that you see everyone else as better than you, or that everybody demands your equal attention, or that they know more than you and are closer to God than you. That is not what seeing the divine in everyone means. It simply means that you recognize that others are divine *and* they are human. You hold this dual perspective, with a deep humility that your opinions and prior experiences may tell you little about them. It means learning to listen without judgment. It means remaining humble as to why this person has shown up in your life. It means remaining kind and gentle, willing to be of service without self-sacrifice. It means not placing expectations on how the other person should be or engaging them with a sense of utility. It means seeing them with a sense of wonder and awe at the possibilities of being that they might embody.

Although everyone is a divine emanation, that does not mean we will create the same depth of relationship with them. Not every relationship is going to lead to the same level of intimacy. That is not a fault. It is not a sign of lack or a testament to your inability to love. We have to make choices about how to spend our time and energy with those who enter our lives. We cannot devote ourselves to each person in the same way that we might devote ourselves to a partner or to our closest friends. We would soon find ourselves spread thin, without any time for ourselves, or find that the time we could give to each person who crosses our path is so little that we devote no meaningful part of our lives to any one of them.

When making such decisions, remember that another's worthiness does not depend on whether you've formed a bond or connection. Instead, bring a sense of reverence for the fact that they are unique creations whose depth of being and purpose in life are not yours to evaluate or judge. After all, you have no idea of the role they have played in countless other lives. You can see each person as an integral piece of the puzzle that makes up the world without needing to know the full picture. You can bring this combination of compassion, benevolence, humility, and dignity to every relationship, reminding your heart that it can remain open to each and every time traveler who intersects your timeline. What role they'll play and how long they'll play it remain to be seen. When we commit ourselves to seeing the stranger through the eyes of the divine, we become angels in human form.

SURRENDER:
YOUR SOUL KNOWS WHAT
THE FUTURE HOLDS

᯾

Despite our desire to remain in the present, the future beckons. Time's passage is inevitable. The future is but a series of present moments that have not yet revealed themselves. Our path of awakening often leads us in pursuit of a future where we are fully realized, where we have released our pain and given birth to so many versions of ourselves that we finally become the authentic self we so desperately desire to embody. But the future is not written. Your trajectory is not fixed. It is full of possibility, uncertainty, and at times, unimaginable pain. How do you face the unknown of the future without falling prey to anxiety? And if you could know in advance all that would happen to you, including tragedy, would you want to know?

This is the conundrum presented by the film *Arrival*. Early on, the protagonist, played by Amy Adams, begins to have what appear to be flashbacks. Snapshots of interactions with a child or family members, presented obscurely, evoke a sense of grief or despair. We think we're seeing her memories. Only later do we discover that Adams was witnessing the future. Those supposed flashbacks reveal that in the future, she and Jeremy Renner, whom she meets when the aliens arrive on the planet, will have a daughter together, their daughter will die from an incurable disease, and they will separate because Renner cannot overcome his grief. These scenes are flashforwards, not flashbacks.

The ability to see glimpses of the future is the lynchpin of the film: Adams solves a riddle in the present by seeing the future moment where she conveys a key message to a war-hungry general who is on the verge of unleashing nuclear weapons to stop what he mistakenly perceives as an alien threat. Using this newfound clairvoyance, Adams utters the message the general needs to hear to stand down, thus averting a global catastrophe. It is at this point that the viewer understands that the images of her child's death and the loss of her husband are prophecies, not memories. Knowing her future does not lead her to try to change it, however. Adams sees the life ahead of her, and she steps wholeheartedly into the pain that awaits.

Although your life may not involve using flashforwards to save humanity from an alien invasion, some part of you may long to access the future. This is the allure of prophecy and prediction. No matter how much we want to remain in the present moment, a part of us can't help but peer toward the future. Where might we end up? We want reassurance that we are on the right path. We seek some measure of solace, even a hint of a guarantee, that we will live a full, happy life and that we will realize who we believe we are meant to be. Our thoughts turn ahead to moments not yet created, often with an undercurrent of worry.

I have yet to meet a spiritual seeker who truly remained present and never thought about the future. I've often wondered if I could know my future in all its rich detail, if I could read through all the chapters of my biography to see where life would take me, would I really want to know? Would I step into that life if I knew the pain that awaited me, or would I attempt to steer clear of it? In truth, I would not want to know. But we all carry within us this voice—sometimes small, other times quite vocal—that wants to be certain that we'll be taken care of, we'll be safe, and we'll have our material needs met. We might be curious about where we'll end up, if we will get to realize our dreams, if we will find love or success or self-realization or whatever it is that we hope lies for us in the future.

That little voice—anxious, worrisome, needy, and clingy—struggles with uncertainty. The possibility of pain, suffering, setback, or worse lurks in the unseen ticks of the clock, waiting to spring forth. If you're prone to anxiety, you might experience this as a deep anxiety that you are doomed to failure or as an inability to rest comfortably when life is going smoothly, as if you were waiting for the other shoe to drop. No matter how much we practice, we eventually fall out of the flow with the present moment and begin to ponder our future, not with the joy of creative possibility, but with the fear of avoiding calamity. Uncertainty sets in.

Our usual approaches to handling uncertainty are the same ones we so often rely on for any kind of emotional discomfort: We run from those feelings or numb ourselves. But the future is a tricky dimension of the mind, and for some it's far easier to push the past aside than it is to keep thoughts of the future at bay. In part, that is because fear is one of the most powerful feelings we have. It is also owed, I think, to the fact that our minds are looking ahead for threats, relying on the past for its guidance. The unknown of the future invites us to worry and speculate far more than the known pain of the past.

The solutions we resort to tend to be efforts to control or predict the future. The same impulse to empire building that drives our desire to stake a claim in this world is often the impulse that wards off the fear of the future. We attempt to wrestle the world to our feet, carving out a space of control in the workplace and in our personal lives. We fight for a piece of the economic pie, building brands, businesses, and careers, and we do our best to avoid the control of other people who likewise attempt to manage their emotions by controlling those who come into their orbit. Or we rely on the predictions of others who claim to know our future. But no matter how large you grow or how many predictions you receive, you will never dispel uncertainty and fear of the future, for you will always fear that it is never enough, that what you have could be lost or taken from you, or that the prediction is wrong.

The path through this temporal dilemma does not lie in controlling or predicting the future, for neither can be done. Instead, we must unwind our penchant to obsess over that which has not yet happened. We must embrace uncertainty, change, and the unknown. We must also relinquish our grip on our need to treat the future as a dimension to be conquered.

One of the lessons that we are often taught is that we must work hard, even fight, for our place at the table; we must struggle, push ourselves, and be better than the rest to achieve our goals. Spirituality is about learning to create your life in concert with the world. You are looking for trust in a world where betrayal appears to be the norm. The universe is not your enemy; it is not something that has to be subdued so that you can stake a flag at the top of some mound of dirt. When you embrace your connection with the divine inside, you learn to create opportunities in different ways. You allow your soul to guide you, trusting in its guidance. The more you let go and allow yourself to be carried, the more control and trust you gain over the direction of your life.

FEAR OF CHANGE

No matter what stage of life you're in, you likely yearn for some part of your life to be different. Especially if you've awakened, you've come to see that you've made choices that were not aligned with your soul, and therefore you now see parts of your life—a job, relationships, commitments you've made—may no longer quite fit this new version of yourself. You start to dream of something else, of new possibilities.

As we open ourselves to other opportunities in life, we inevitably confront our fear of change. Human beings are burdened by this deeply contradictory impulse: We so very much want our lives to be different, but we fear charting a new course. We are not satisfied with the present. We desire change, but only if we can guarantee that it'll be for the better. We worry that any changes we make will be *for the worse*. We can manage the familiar dangers, but the unknown ones cause us to worry about our survival.

That's a not very subtle way of making everyone else the problem, for the only real solution if we don't change is for everyone else to conform to our wishes and thereby make our lives different. In other words, if you aren't satisfied in your job, relationship, living situation, etc., and you refuse to change, you're essentially expecting that your coworkers, significant other, neighbors, etc., will modify their behavior to make you happy. That, of course, is what empire-building egos seek to do; they make everyone else do things their way. There's only one way out of this conundrum: You have to accept wholeheartedly where you are and be at peace with it, or you can make a change and ride the wave of emotions that comes with the transition from one life to another.

As we have already seen in Chapter 1, it's essential that you accept your circumstances and explore your feelings of dissatisfaction. If you don't truly know why you are dissatisfied, and you try to change your external circumstances to gain satisfaction, that satisfaction may be short-lived. Very often we change external situations in hopes of resolving some internal dissatisfaction. People make changes hoping to find a place where they feel they belong or to connect with a group of like-minded colleagues. They move on to a new job, and after the so-called honeymoon period ends, the same struggles with other people reemerge. The struggles with the workplace that you fled get mirrored again through other people because what you need to face is your internal dissatisfaction. Until you face that directly, you will keep chasing external circumstances that you hope and believe will make you happy but never do.

If you decide that change is the right course of action, yet resist taking action, you must confront your fear of change. The problem with change is that it is tinged with uncertainty. The unknown is our great fear, for the unknown presents the possibility of failure, suffering, and worst of all, death. Uncertainty is the ego's way of painting possibilities with a paintbrush of fear. It takes infinite possibilities and highlights the negative ones, and in so doing, obscures the vast positive potential of the unlived moment.

Change also requires effort. It's true that change demands that we focus our energies and opt for something new. Years ago, when I wanted to leave my academic position for the law, I had to prepare for the law school entrance exams, craft applications, gather letters of recommendation, and attend interviews. It was an enormous amount of work. Similarly, when I was finished with law school and experiencing a spiritual awakening that led me to explore my inner world and connection with the divine, I had to put in considerable effort to meditate, pray, recite mantras, read works of spiritual wisdom, and work with different teachers. Forging a new path required effort. Sometimes it is our resistance or lack of energy that keeps us where we are.

Often, though, even that resistance is tied in some way to fear, particularly a fear of failure. What is the antidote to this way of seeing the world through danger-tinged glasses? Begin by accepting the truth that change is inevitable. Our bodies grow old, other people change and move away, new creations emerge, older creations pass on. There is no stasis. The passage of time charted by our linear minds means that we cannot avoid transition and transformation. Change happens whether we want it to or not. That is a lesson those who have experienced a dark night of the soul know well. Embracing this truth can soften our grip that holds onto a present that is already gone. You cannot hold onto time, so even if you were to attempt to stay in the same job, maintain the same relationship, live in the same place, those areas of your life would continue to change.

Next, you must step into your fear. The journey to a new future leads to the past, for you must get to the root of your fear that you will fail. Whether deep down or close to the surface, you feel that you're not good enough or won't have enough. You fear that someone will undermine or harm you, take your piece of the pie. You've probably experienced failures, losses, setbacks, abuses, or even profound tragedies. Those experiences, and the emotions that accompany them, are not to be denied, but did you survive? The fact that you are reading these words right now is a testament to your resilience.

Very often what holds us back from change is a sense of regret, the feeling that we've made mistakes and we don't want to be burned again. That's a normal and understandable response to some of the pain that we've all faced. Maybe you took a chance—on a career, on a relationship—and it didn't pan out. Your psyche may have been seared with hot memories of rejection, embarrassment, shame, or feeling like a failure. Now you're looking not to repeat them. That's sound advice if you did something that caused you a lot of pain and can learn the lesson you were meant to learn. Maybe you tried to get away with something—some deceit or harm—and got caught. Maybe you took a risk with a new venture, business, or another enterprise, and it "failed." Did you see your experience as a learning opportunity where you gained valuable lessons, or did you see the event as life smacking you in the face?

Your fears are not rational, and they don't respond to reason. They get triggered, like a fight or flight response; a portion of your brain dedicated to survival is still on high alert. You have to embrace that pain, feel it, and give it permission to be experienced and released. Learn the lessons of those events, rather than simply looking to avoid their repetition in the future. The hard work of awareness, acceptance, and forgiveness that has occupied so many of these pages must be brought to bear on this deeply rooted fear. That is the painstaking work we all must do to see ourselves in a different light—to come back to the vision of the soul—and recognize that these events can be imbued with a new interpretation, a different meaning. We practice resurrection so that we can face the future without it being shaped by the lens of the past.

One of the most beautiful and uplifting practices you can undertake to dispel regret is to review all the episodes in your life that turned out to be blessings in disguise. Look back over your life and consider how time has shifted your perspective on what once seemed like the most tragic of events. You might recall the Zen parable of "Maybe" that we discussed earlier. Somewhere you suffered a setback, loss, or disappointment.

At the time, it felt like the universe was letting you down, or worse, conspiring against you. Yet with the benefit of time, you could later see that this event's unfolding became the condition that gave rise to something else even more positive. Countless people have lost their jobs and homes only to realize that the loss paved the way to something far greater than they could have imagined. All of this is a reminder that as you approach change with trepidation or worry, whatever setback or minor stumbling you face on this uncertain journey will later, in time, be revealed for its fortune. Holding onto the conviction despite the fear you now feel is what it means to trust life.

By reflecting on your prior moments of fear and how they gave way eventually to peace, you might come to realize that you are far stronger and more resilient than you've known. You might simply gain some fortitude in recognizing your capacity to weather adversity and move through fear, failure, and other moments of regret. Once you've released this pain, your body might be more at ease in stepping into fear again. We can learn to be comfortable with the discomfort of the unknown.

Years ago, as I sat in my very first class in law school, surrounded by my fellow first-year law students, panic suddenly washed over me. I had never felt such intense fear before, but it blazed through me, scorching my entire body. Sweat oozed from my pores, and my breathing quickened. It lasted maybe five minutes and was done. The panic happened at the precise moment that I realized there was no turning back. Just a few weeks prior, I had left my job at Northwestern University, where I was on the verge of tenure, packed up my belongings, and moved from Chicago to New York. I was thirty-four, a decade older than your average law student. I had walked away from security for an entirely new adventure. I won't sugarcoat it: Law school was *demanding*. It's a grueling experience for anybody, but for me, it was compounded by my decision to give up a tenure-track job.

Every change presents an opportunity to learn a lesson—sometimes a painful one—in loss, rejection, or failure. There was no way for me to be a lawyer and live my life the same way I had been. I had to pack up, move, and start my life over. I had to feel a lot of fear along the way. I have never regretted making that change, notwithstanding that initial panic attack. Law school, and the career that followed, turned out to be wonderful.

As you make changes and move through fear, you will soon notice how cyclical fear is. It is always rising and falling. One moment you feel fine, at peace with your move, and the next seems to invite a tidal wave of anxiety. With each new leap you start to see the familiar pattern of your mind whispering anxiously to pause. *Let's wait a bit more*, it says. You can, each time, unwind that voice by continuing to embrace the present moment, even if the circumstances are unfamiliar to you. You must learn to recognize that each wave will attempt to convince you that it is right; that even though you've survived those other waves, this one will be the one that drowns you.

One trick I like to use is to give fear an image, an identity, and a voice: I try to imagine my fear, whenever it speaks to me, as Whoopi Goldberg from *Ghost* when she tells Demi Moore, "You in danger, gurl!" The humor in that image makes my fear seem a lot less ferocious and more playful. You can also remind yourself of your reasons for leaving behind an old life. We often very quickly forget the downsides and the reasons for leaving. The familiarity, safety, and security of an old life eventually resurface, singing their siren song.

Once I became a lawyer, there were moments when I longed for my academic life, teaching three days a week, with summers off. When I was working sixty-hour weeks, racing to court, filing briefs, etc., I looked back on my academic life with nostalgia. But I also remember the times I stared at a room of students who had no interest in being there, or listened to colleagues drone on in a faculty meeting about a trivial administrative matter. I had to focus instead on the parts that I loved. Noodling through a complex legal issue, appearing in court, and feeling the satisfaction of a client's gratitude were among the high points.

Another technique is to look back at the transitions you've weathered and ponder your older self from this present vantage point. You may find yourself marveling at why the transition seemed so daunting or reveling with gratitude in where you are now. Transitions, while bringing a lot of uncertainty with them, also contain with them the potential for magic and wonder. The funny thing about navigating change and the accompanying fear is that, each time, your fear will tell you that *this time* the danger is real. *This time* the change won't be good for you. *This time* the failure will be devastating. It's helpful to remind yourself that these feelings—and the voice of doom—are familiar. You've been here before. Your mind will tell you that it won't work out, that you're facing certain doom and it would be better to stay put. Fear is a terrible psychic. It rarely predicts the future with any accuracy.

* * *

Embracing uncertainty requires you to perceive the future through a different lens. Rather than focusing on the negative potential of the future, what if you could shift your view to one of awe, wonder, and mystery? What good or amazing possibilities might unfold, including ones you have never thought feasible? Remember what it was like as a child to let your imagination roam. Did you live a life of fantasy? Did you look forward to adventures with friends? Did you imagine a future filled with excitement? Notice whether you did all of this with a kind of abandon, where it was all delight and little fear, with no questions of how you might pay for it, whether people would approve, or if you would fail. So often, when we are young, we can access this imaginative faculty without our world-weariness stomping on our joy.

Opening ourselves to wonder inspires a conscious and deliberate shift in feeling. You cultivate an openness to options you might not even be aware of with a feeling of excitement. It's like saying to the universe, *I like this menu, but what else is there, off the menu?* You're asking for life to surprise and delight you, rather than school you with more painful lessons. You're learning to treat your life with the same kind of joy that you bring to your entertainment. Do you like to jump ahead to the end of a book or movie or skip episodes in a television series and go straight to the finale? I don't. I might be riddled with impatience and itchy with anticipation, but I love not knowing the outcome and relish watching the decisions that our favorite characters make, cringing when they repeat the same "mistakes" and don't see their own patterns that seem as clear as day to us, the viewers. Why shouldn't our own lives inspire the same kind of mystery, awe, and delight?

Opening ourselves to the wonder of the universe is not an easy task, but it starts by embracing the mystery of the present moment. Pregnant with multiple possibilities, each second is a portal to a new dimension. Each moment offers you an array of choices for what you will create with the gift that the moment affords you. That's the power of sovereignty, to choose your life. That's the joy of uncertainty—the path ahead is not fixed. You may have more or fewer choices in any given moment based on prior choices. Prior choices may have shaped what lies before you, but they don't determine the next step. You always have more choices than you realize, including how you react to all that is unfolding in your life. The question you must ask yourself is, *What will I choose to create with this moment?*

LISTENING TO YOUR INTUITION

If you embrace the truth that not every change sends you plummeting toward disaster, you can release the energy of fear that you have bottled up inside. You start to see change as exciting because you know that change is not dangerous—and it's also unavoidable. Your life is a testament to that fact. From there, you can open to the unknown as a rich possibility for experiencing something new, something fresh, or a new way of being. You forge a new kind of confidence that life will support you through even the direst of circumstances. The unknown sheds its fearful veneer.

There's a word for this new stage of confidence: trust. Trust happens incrementally. Fear wanes, but does it disappear entirely? After a series of rather dramatic and downright magical awakenings, including my kundalini awakening, transformed me into a psychic channel, I left my life in the law to pursue a living as a spiritual writer and intuitive. But even having weathered a transition from literature to law, I *still* resisted the change. I hemmed and hawed and tried to negotiate with my guides, who were insistent it was time to move on. I took the leap, and life has been magical again in its own ways. Have I experienced failure? For sure. Have I had moments of regret or pangs of worry that life would have been better, easier, or more lucrative as a lawyer? Of course. But I have also had tremendous experiences I would never have had if I had continued to work as a litigator, and I never have had a panic attack like I did when I moved from literature to law.

This is the cultivation of trust. You slowly build a relationship with yourself and your life where you do not meet the world with suspicion or believe it is your antagonist. This path begins by trusting yourself, and to do that you must develop a relationship with your inner guidance. That voice inside, which is an expression of the divine inside, is your intuition.

We all yearn to hear that little voice of divine guidance, even though it is not always easy to detect. It can be subtle, like a whisper. It's easy to drown out with mental chatter, internet, music, and banter. That's because it's not always a voice, exactly. Sometimes it's an impulse or a tug, in one direction or another, one so quick that you might miss it if you're rushing through your day. You have to hone it over the years by making an effort to listen and be guided. Learning to recognize the differences between fear and desire, on the one hand, and the gentle urging of your intuition, on the other, is not easy.

The first step is to learn to recognize the ways that your intuition speaks to you. It's different for each person, but there are three common ways your intuition will often make itself heard. Sometimes we feel fear or anxiety about a situation, but other times, as my cautionary tale from Chapter 6 suggests, you can sense danger despite the absence of any visible threat. How do you know if it's fear or intuition? In my case, I hear my intuition warning me of danger deep in my gut, and after honing my intuition over the years, I now hear it audibly. It starts as a dull warning, and then it gets stronger and more nauseating the longer I ignore it. Sometimes it's just a sense of knowing that something is off or wrong—avoiding a certain street, an event, an item of food. I can feel my body recoil. By contrast, for me, fear is very much in my chest and the upper region of my body. Very often I'll hear my ego say something, and I distinguish it from my intuition because it's a whinier, more judgmental voice. Then I know that my resistance to something is based on an old pattern, my mind reacting to what it perceives as danger.

That same intuitive voice can pull you toward some kind of action, even one that might seem irrational. It's like a tiny little bell, something that just "pops into your head" but feels right. If you don't learn to hear it, you'll barely notice the thought and move on to something else. Years ago, while I was still working as a lawyer, I was doing work on environmental law in my spare time. One day, I felt quite clever in having come up with the phrase "carbon karma" to describe one's impact on the environment. As I was leaving work, though, I felt that familiar tug and heard that I should follow the prompts. My intuition led me on a stroll through the city, telling me to go left, turn right, etc. It led me to a block I didn't know in Midtown Manhattan, to a small cafe. I walked inside and posted on their menu was a mission statement that talked about reducing one's "carbon karma." My intuition had led me on a trip to show me that my phrase was not original.

The path to hearing this voice requires you to create space in your mind for it. Meditation is the primary way to allow your normal mental chatter to subside so that you can distinguish your ego from your intuition. Listening to that inner voice is different from listening to the ego, with its whiny, petulant, or caustic tone. For me, my intuition is softer and gentler, and unless it is calling me to avoid danger, it is always affirmative. I have meditated for over a decade, and I am now very familiar with that voice, also known as clairaudience. If I don't meditate, the ego will override it, ignore it, or otherwise censor it. Clairaudience isn't the only intuitive skill. Sometimes you'll just know information (claircognizance), or you'll feel something about someone else's physical or emotional state (clairsentience).

It's important to distinguish between a true intuitive hit and a projection based on your own biases or emotions. It's easy to confuse and conflate your personal stuff with what you think is intuitive guidance. You may need to test your knowledge by verifying it from another source, because along the way you will *think* you know, but you may just be responding to your ego's patterns rather than genuinely connecting with your intuition. As you practice with verification, you'll develop confidence in your intuition and trust it more each time.

Another way to develop your intuition as a tool you can trust is to start small and let your intuition guide you in small ways. One way I've practiced this is by letting my intuition guide me when I'm traveling. Allow your intuition to tell you to go down one street or another, to take a route you might never have taken otherwise. If you live in a city with public transportation, allow it to pick which subway car to take. Another option is to ask your intuition to pick something off the menu for you when you're ordering food. Set the intention to let your intuitive abilities either show you what something will taste like or ask to be surprised with something you wouldn't order but might enjoy and see if your expectations are met. Even if you get it wrong and don't get an intuitive hit, or get something that you regret, the cost is just one dish or meal. With these steps, you develop confidence in your capacity to hear your intuition accurately, so when you start to bring it to bear on more significant decisions, you can trust it.

The practice of self-forgiveness is one of the most powerful ways to hear your intuition. You may be surprised by this suggestion, but self-forgiveness tells your inner voice that you will listen to it. Very often we don't hear our intuition because we're so used to hearing the ego's internal voice of reproach. We hold ourselves accountable, often to impossible standards. That voice tends to drown out the more subtle tones of your intuition. By practicing self-forgiveness, you are detaching from a prior moment where you are still judging yourself. And letting go of judgment—which comes from attachment to the way you think things *should* be—is a critical aspect of learning to listen to your intuition. People easily become attached to outcomes. How else are you going to be open to information that doesn't make rational sense if you are constantly judging yourself and the world around you by expecting it to be a certain way?

Hearing your intuition is one of the most natural and joyous experiences you can have. We all have intuitive abilities, and while some more than others are in touch with them, everyone can deepen their connection to their intuition and feel more divinely guided in everyday life.

As you deepen your intuition, learning to hear the call of your soul through gentle whispers and tugs of the gut, you will also begin to see signs in the external world. After all, you are one with the universe, so the physical world around you will begin to shower you with signs and suggestions consistent with the impulses of the heart. Those might show up as messages that seem to be exactly what you needed at a given moment. A book, an individual, an article, a reminder of some kind will gently lead you forward. You might start to dive into some of the more esoteric avenues around signs and synchronicity, such as the role of repeating numbers. If those resonate with you and provide you a sense of guidance and comfort, then rely on them. But as with any information, trust your inner guidance and experience above all. You can, of course, always ask for more direct signs, for the message of where you need to go or what you need to do to be spelled out more plainly for you. This is part of the dialogue of cocreation with your soul. The ways in which your soul speaks to you, how the universe might dialogue with you, is part of your unique relationship to it. You need not attempt to model that dialogue on what others have said about numbers, signs, and synchronicity. It's enough to be open to however those messages might show up.

SURRENDERING TO LIFE

Once you've strengthened this connection with your own divine guidance, then you can open to each moment of the unknown with the belief, rooted in trust, that life is leading you always to growth, opportunity, and flourishing. When you let go and allow yourself to be carried, life can sometimes feel like a rollercoaster: You know that you're held in place, strapped in tight, and yet the twists and turns can still be exhilarating. That's how you start cocreating with your soul—by allowing yourself to be led. Only then will you come to discover treasures and worlds that you never imagined were possible because you gave up focusing solely on ensuring a future that was safe and familiar. The ego will delight for a bit and then feel some fear, as if to warn that this next step might be dangerous. The line between excitement and fear is a thin one. Embrace the uncertainty and let the universe take you on the ride of your life.

There is a tendency in spiritual circles to reinvent the ego's efforts to create change by presenting that work as a kind of spiritual practice under the guise of "manifestation." A sense of control slips in, as if you might cajole the universe with a big enough vision board to give you what you want. Of course, there's nothing wrong with having intention and focus. They are, in fact, crucial to living the life you desire, as long as you know what you want and *why* you want it—and therein lies the rub: So much of what people still desire has more to do with assuaging their egos than living in alignment with their souls. You can hold to a vision but notice above all the feeling that it inspires in you. Is it a sense of relief under which you can detect a deep sense of lack or frustration? Is it a sense of expansion and joy? Is it a feeling of connection and creativity? Only you can know how it feels to be aligned with your soul. Create room for your soul's movement by concentrating on the feeling that you want to experience. Then ask for your soul to lead and take over.

Surrender flows from trust. Surrender is the stage where you really know who you are, and your trust is so deep that you let go of the oars of manifesting, knowing that you are manifesting all the time in concert with the divine. Set the intention to be open to receiving what you need. This has been my path to finding the life that truly enlivens me and makes me feel the most authentic. I have learned that my soul is a much better captain on the choppy sea waters of life than I am. The greatest joys and gifts of my life have appeared not because I envisioned them with clear descriptions mapped out on vision boards, but because I asked my soul to show me some aspect of life I was missing.

Setting the intention to be led by your soul is, in essence, a form of prayer. Prayer is a heartfelt request for an answer that lies beyond you, and thus is always an act of surrender when you do not dictate what the outcome should be. When you pray in this way, you create a space of allowance for the world to shift in a way that you do not control and cannot anticipate. Sometimes we fall into the habit of using prayer in a controlling way. We start to use it as a get-out-of-jail-free card; when a situation doesn't make us happy, or we're desperate, we turn to prayer. It's our trump card when we think the hand we're dealt is a losing one. We have made prayer a tool when our normal efforts at ruling the world and getting our way seem to fail us. That's not how prayer works. It's not about getting what you want or desperate measures in the face of some major calamity.

Prayer will work in those situations, but most often only when you've cultivated that sense of truth that you and the divine are always cocreating together. Prayer as an instrument of surrender is meant to be used on a regular basis to create an intimate dialogue between you and the universe, for there is no true separation between you. Prayer is one way of invoking the energy of creation. You pray when you set an intention without knowing what the outcome should look like or how best to realize your goal. The best prayer always surrenders to an outcome that is for the highest good of all parties who are involved, whatever form that may take. The outcome may not be what you anticipated or hoped for, but undoubtedly, at a future moment, you will look back and see once again that whatever transpired was a blessing in disguise.

Because we are energetic beings, being carried is itself an act of surrender because you release your expectations. You can keep the intention, though, of knowing yourself and feeling gratitude, joy, and wonder, but they become even more untethered from the dictates of the ego or the experiences you've already had. When you surrender, you create an openness in you for possibilities that aren't remotely on your radar.

* * *

Even when we have experienced the ecstasy of our soul and the sweetness of surrender, we also run afoul of a certain pitfall:

believing that we've reached a certain stage, as if we had graduated from one grade to the next. As we deepen our connection to the divine inside, we tend to fall prey to linear thinking. We fear, then trust, then surrender, and the rest is bliss. But sometimes when we've learned to handle more, the universe places a much bigger challenge in our way. Growth is not linear, and it doesn't look like we expect it to. This is where control and expectation sneak in the side door of our psyches.

I've had to manage this many times as I stepped further and further onto my path. The mind says that we've given in and surrendered to the path, and now begs to understand why this path isn't easy or why our lives aren't unfolding with boundless bliss and effortless manifestation. We compare who we are now with who we were before, and we decide whether we have declined or improved. We judge ourselves if fear returns, our trust wanes, or we fall out of a state of surrender into older patterns. We flog ourselves for what we perceive as backsliding. In truth, we need to release our perception that every moment must be positive simply because we have healed so much of our past pain.

Surrender is not always about being carried toward positive experiences. Sometimes, we learn that surrender happens when life decides that a certain change is necessary. This can feel a bit like a version of the dark night of the soul. Even after you've awakened and you think you're following your guidance, the universe might intervene if you're not really listening. That can happen with a sudden loss of a job, or when a relationship shifts. These might be pieces of your life that you didn't want to change even as you pursue your spiritual journey. Sometimes the plan doesn't obey exactly what you want, and life forces you to shift in unanticipated and undesired ways. It can feel like you're being pushed, not carried, because you've been resisting your intuition and the signs from your soul that you needed to make a change.

This is a different kind of surrender: No matter how tightly you cling to what you already know or have, the waters of life won't let you hold on. To surrender to the divine is to allow yourself to cocreate not according to the whims of the ego but to the wishes of the soul. The more you allow your intuition to guide you, the more easily it will take you where you need to go. You will learn that you have the power to choose paths that are less bumpy. Not every lesson needs to be learned through pain. Each step happens more fluidly, with less hesitation. There's a certainty that underlies your actions even when the outcome is not clear. When you surrender, you are infused with the faith that life is not a journey of fear but a dance to the music of the soul. All it takes is the willingness to listen.

DEATH:
YOUR TIME IS FINITE AND ETERNAL

⫸

E VEN THOUGH THE future is not yet written and we learn to surrender our efforts to control the world around us, there is one guarantee in life: Our time here will end. No matter how much we strive to step out of time—to be in the present and not the imaginary ruminations of the future—linear time, with an endpoint, cannot be avoided.

For some, death is welcomed. It was 2003, and I had traveled to Northern California to see my great-grandmother. She was in her eighties, and she was quite frail. I was worried that it would be the last time I would see her. It turns out I was right: When I arrived, I learned that she had decided to stop eating, and she was far thinner than the last time I had seen her. She explained that she had lived a long life and was tired. She could no longer do the things she most loved to do—travel the world, hike, and photograph nature. She had been an avid photographer of nature for many years as she traveled the globe, hiking and exploring, but her body no longer had the energy. After years of being homebound, she no longer found joy in daily life. She decided that it was time to face death, and by choosing not to eat, she was hastening the process. She felt complete, she said, and no longer wanted to be in her body. A few weeks after our visit, she passed away.

For others, death comes as a shock. It was January 2018, and my friend Sally had come back to New York from Charleston, South Carolina, where she now lived and worked. She told me about a lump that was diagnosed initially as a benign tissue growth and then osteosarcoma—bone cancer. Tears spilled freely as we talked about what that likely meant. Bone cancer is almost always fatal. An entrepreneurial and fearless advocate for social justice, Sally had started her own nonprofit legal practice to serve those whose income wasn't enough to pay for a private lawyer but was still too high to receive the services of legal aid designed for the poor. Her life was turned upside down for the next year and a half with countless infusions of chemotherapy that wrecked her kidneys and radiation treatments that left chunks of skin falling off. Her body was now in constant pain and fatigue. Sally had so much more to give to this world and wanted to live, yet the cancer in her bones, which then spread to her lymph nodes, refused to budge. She died a year and a half later.

* * *

Through these two beloved relationships, death reminded me that it does not bend to our wishes. We hope, like my grandmother, to live a full life and feel complete, and we fear, like my friend, that death will arrive sooner than expected. My grandmother wanted death to come, yet it delayed until she starved her body. My friend wanted to live longer, but death refused to stand down, despite all the efforts to sustain her body. We can take care of our bodies, exercise, rest, and eat well. We can make plans or decide not to do much of anything. Death has its own timetable.

In both cases, death brought with it an intimacy and

honesty about life that we often seek and cannot find. For my grandmother, the imminence of her death meant that she opened up to me in a way that she never had, telling me stories about raising my mother, her first and second marriages, and how much she loved me. For my friend Sally, she was forced to be taken care of, to receive the kind of support she had so often given to others, and she was able to open up to me about her fear around death and what might come after, a topic that we had never broached before. Death has a way of loosening our hearts and giving us the courage to reveal ourselves before time runs out. It gives life an urgency and meaning that our focus on day-to-day matters can obscure.

Few of us face death voluntarily. Instead, we allow the omnipresent fear of death to shape and mold our lives, often unconsciously. Herein lies our fundamental predicament: We can only be in the present moment, the one that exists, but the number of our present moments is finite. Our death is guaranteed. It is the one experience all of us are destined to have. Despite the fact that death is so profoundly entwined with our lives, we resist facing it.

We almost always face death only when we are forced to, when illness or injury suddenly imposes itself upon us, or when we must grieve the loss of our loved ones. When we are young, we feel like we'll live forever; we have so little sense of how fast time will pass. When we are adults, we worry about the future and our death, so much so that we often are not present to how fast time is passing. We cannot imagine that we would want to speed up time, that we'd want to be done here on the planet. We want more time. When my grandmother said she didn't want to spend more time here, it was not a sentiment I could understand; I was in my early thirties, excited about life's adventures. Until these moments, when death demands we pay attention, rarely do we allow ourselves to contemplate death or feel our fear of it.

As daunting as it sounds, the spiritual path asks you to welcome death, not fear it. Death offers a sense of completion and finality that, in turn, gives life a tenderness and sweetness it would otherwise lack. We need death, even if we often don't appreciate how much we need it until the end of our lives, when the pain and toil to our bodies makes remaining here a burden. Finding ways to remind yourself of the omnipresence of death is not morbid at all. Instead, it is one of the most powerful portals to seeing the world through the eyes of love.

WHY WE FEAR DEATH

To say that we fear our death is hardly a profound insight. A deeply embedded survival instinct has propelled our evolution; our bodies know more about keeping us alive than we realize. Yet we quickly learn as children how fragile we are, and we spend much of our lives safeguarding against harm and fretting about our security. The pain of that truth becomes a constant companion in life, so much so that parents often struggle with how to handle questions of death when their children first begin to pose them. From a very early age, we are implanted with the belief that life is precarious and the world full of threats to our survival. Nearly every negative emotion that we experience can be traced back, at its core, to our fundamental fear of death. The end of time shapes our relationship to the world.

There's a wonderful irony that a future event that we cannot control and cannot possibly anticipate casts such a long shadow over our lives. There is no escaping the truth of death. The irony is that the very quality that gives us the capacity of being human—our perception of time—is what allows for us to fear death by being aware of its possibility. We can see the future—only one aspect of the future—and that is that there will be a point where we cease to be. Death and life are integral because they are fundamentally part of separation. Being human means that we perceive ourselves as separate from others, with a distinct existence in time and space. That sense of separation gives rise to our perception of time, and also our fear of death. Time gives rise to the possibility of death, that there would be an end to our time. Thus, our very lives depend on a concept that by its nature carries within it the seeds of its own annihilation. In that regard, death is part of life in this very moment. The moment you experience now is instantly gone; that moment has passed, and you are in a new present moment. That flash of time is, in a sense, dead, because it is now reduced to memory.

But it is equally human to avoid fear and pain, and we tend to respond to our fear of death in the same way we handle most of our emotions—we suppress it. The funny thing about our fear of death is that it is rife with contradiction, and those contradictions become inescapable when we start to look at the ways we manage this fear.

One of the most common ways of suppressing our fear of death is to make ourselves larger and more visible. Fame and celebrity become antidotes to close cousins of death: invisibility, obscurity, and loneliness. Yet, as anybody who has embraced fame knows, being seen so that you'll be remembered also means that you're exposed. Your physical safety is even more precarious. The effort to make yourself visible, to leave your mark on the world, means that you end up courting more threats from the world. Any celebrity or politician will tell you that it is impossible to understand the loss of anonymity until you've experienced it yourself. Making yourself famous does little to ward off the fear of death.

Until we face our fear of death, we will be preoccupied with our physical safety. We will see the world through the dingy frame of threat and security, worrying and attempting to exert a certain kind of control over it. That means moving through power, manipulation, and exertion so that everyone around you is kept in check in some way. We see this in our social anxieties around security, borders, barriers, and other ways of self-protection. We control our fear of death by attempting to control the means by which death might reach us through other people. Our constant political battles over privacy, freedom, surveillance, and security all play out this tension around attempting to control in order to ward off death. Yet there is only so much control you can exert. You can go in the opposite direction of fame and seek invisibility, isolation, and anonymity. You can make yourself as small as possible in the hope of avoiding conflict. In the end, neither making yourself larger and more visible, nor making yourself smaller and invisible, are antidotes to our fear.

The reason for this is quite simple: Our fear of death is not so much the fear of the physical perishing of our bodies, although we often experience a lot of fear and distress about the possibility of a long and painful death. Instead, our fear of death is that we do not know what comes after. This is the ultimate unknown, that which we cannot anticipate or know in advance. The ultimate unknown thus becomes our ultimate fear.

THE AFTERLIFE

What comes after death has been the subject of speculation and theory as long as humanity has pondered the meaning of life. Religion, spirituality, and atheism have all promoted beliefs about life after death and whether our consciousness survives, and in what form. Stories of near-death experiences are often painted with similar brushstrokes: a sense of peace, a connection with a higher power, an absence of fear, a sense of wholeness, an awareness of a journey to a next phase.

If you are anything like me, you have the conviction that we are eternal spirit, a soul, a spark of God living in human form. That part of us might be eternal, but I do not know what kind of consciousness transcends death. I can't share an experience of it, and I'm not sure it's an experience that we can comprehend while in our physical bodies. Whatever our convictions, we can only hold them with faith. What I do know is that believing that life continues after death does little to dispel my fear of it.

I remember listening to a Zen priest many years ago answer a question about what Buddhism had to say about death, and she replied, "I don't know. I haven't died." Her point was grounded in the Zen focus on direct experience of life. The truth is that we cannot know death until we experience it for ourselves, like so many other facets of human life; intellectual theory and description are poor substitutes for direct experience. How do we explain the mystery of the end of life when none of us can claim the experience of dying and not returning? And in the absence of a direct experience we cannot have, how do we touch our fears around death, perhaps gently, so that we might come to see death as an integral part of life, as something not to be feared but honored?

Each of us must determine for ourselves where our fear of death lies and how deep it runs. Only then can we decide for ourselves how this relationship to death will mold our relationship to life.

We first have to acknowledge what seems most painful to admit: how much death already surrounds us and the degree to which we keep it at bay. Our news is filled with stories about death, even when we are not facing a pandemic, yet somehow this does not alleviate our fear; more often, it exacerbates it, as if it were there to remind us of our deep fragility and insecurity in a malevolent and scary world. At the same time, we fetishize youth and vitality in magazines, celebrity culture, and film. By contrast with indigenous cultures, in the United States we often treat our elders with disregard, not reverence. It seems like every day a new beauty product is announced that will slow the visible signs of aging.

As a society, we revile death, but we also inflict so much of it. Many jurisdictions still have the death penalty. We incarcerate people and lock them up. We deny them, and many others, the capacity to live their lives fully. Historically, we moved cemeteries far away and treat them not as places of reverence, but as spaces of fear and nightmarish stories about ghosts. Our cultural engagement with death betrays our fear by indulging magical or technological fantasies of escaping death, by granting immortality or finding a fountain of youth, by uploading one's consciousness to some computer server or allowing consciousness to be transferred from one cloned body to the next.

At the other end of the spectrum is the fear that death is not final. It reflects our understanding that escaping death is not natural, and in fact, isn't the least bit desirable. This comes out in the role of zombies and vampires, the creatures who cannot be killed and somehow keep returning. Deep down, we know that escaping death is itself a form of death sentence. In *Interview with a Vampire*, Brad Pitt's character Louis describes how immortality and never growing old ultimately deprives life of any joy. Similarly, the young vampire played by Kirsten Dunst realizes that she will always be a child and never grow into an adult and finds that predicament maddening. There's a reason that all of these creatures consume the living, for the escape of true death can only come at the expense of another's life. Escaping death means robbing life of itself.

Our anxieties about death, as portrayed in film, are a symptom of the fact that in the United States we don't honor death in a positive way. By contrast with other cultures who have well-developed rituals for mourning, we tend to avoid the topic in this country. Most often, death makes its way into our consciousness through news stories about large-scale tragedies. Tragedies—death on a massive scale—are devastating events that can nevertheless serve the purpose of awakening you to how deeply your fear of death shapes you. Terrorism, catastrophe, war, or famine bring into our consciousness death on a scale and speed that often leaves us devastated, because we can no longer deny the truth that our physical well-being is quite fragile. Often the response is an outpouring of compassion, driven by the realization that none of us is truly safe. If used consciously, tragedies can impress upon us the value of keeping death in our awareness. They serve as reminders of the fragility of life. Death calls for us to examine it, up close and personal, to get intimate with our fear, and to look at the ways that the differences we have constructed in our world to divide and separate ourselves from each other often contribute to the fragility of life.

TALKING ABOUT DEATH

If large-scale tragedy does not have an emotional impact, death touches most of us deeply when it takes away our loved ones. When my friend Sally revealed her diagnosis of bone cancer, we did not talk about facing death. We talked about treatment and percentages, knowing that the likelihood of success was quite low. When someone close to you is diagnosed with an illness, particularly something as grave as cancer, talk of death is often taken off the table. It doesn't happen by consensus. Our impulse toward life instinctively steers us to positive outcomes and new treatments. It's one of the ways we avoid our fear of death.

Nevertheless, whether a person is facing a terminal illness or simply reaching an advanced age, there will come a time when you can no longer avoid talking about death. Sometimes death is so imminent that there is no time to figure out how to talk about it comfortably. Nevertheless, after months upon months of excruciating chemotherapy and radiation treatments, Sally and I talked, and I could tell right away this call would be different. She said she was tired and wanted to talk about death. I knew that her symptoms and pain were worse than ever, and there were signs of new cancer growth.

I didn't give her the normal cheerleader boost, pushing aside the topic to avoid my discomfort. We spoke through tears, in fits and starts, with lots of pauses filled with sadness and silence. She talked about facing her mortality and the fear that it inspired. She asked me about my beliefs of life after death. I knew there was nothing that I could say that would dispel her fear or provide certainty. All that mattered was my willingness to listen and share when she asked a question.

Death reminds us of our ultimate aloneness, our separation in this world. One of the painful yet poignant lessons of life is we can never fully accompany someone as they face death. It is a journey whose final step we take alone, even if others are with us. After that deeply emotional talk, Sally and I resumed our normal communication, and she kept me updated on her treatment. Some months later, her activity on social media dropped off suddenly. She texted me to come visit. I knew this would be my last one.

We spent most of our time watching television or chatting.

Sally slept a lot, as she had very little energy. In between, I did things like run errands for her and her family or clean the house. Despite her profound fatigue, we spent as much of her awake time together as possible. Throughout the five days of my final visit, I felt this strong urge to touch my friend, aware that the opportunities to hug or hold each other's hands were quickly fading. Most of the time, though, she was in deep pain, and being touched just added to her discomfort.

On our final night, about twenty minutes before I had to head back to my hotel room to get ready for an early flight home, she grabbed my hand and said she was going to hold it until I left. I was so grateful. I knew she was uncomfortable, and in that gesture she was saying everything that we hadn't had an opportunity to say. It was a gesture that said, "I love you," "Goodbye," and "Our friendship means more than the pain I'm in right now." And I held her hand, as gently and as long as I could.

That's essentially all you can do when someone close to you is dying. Holding their hand takes so many forms. It might mean getting them something to drink, helping them to the bathroom, driving them to the hospital, finding some article of clothing, or adjusting the room's temperature. It might mean reading books about death and talking about what we believe happens afterward.

After I returned home from that final visit, I had to step back and let go of checking in on my friend. She had less and less energy each day and many other people waiting to say goodbye. She let me know at a certain point that she could no longer text. Holding my friend's hand also meant realizing when it was time to let go so that she could do what she needed in her remaining time. Sally died peacefully in the middle of August 2019 as her husband read to her.

FACING YOUR FEAR OF DEATH

Once we have lost someone, we learn the intimate dance of grief and mourning. We learn to be with the pain of loss until it fades, and we are left with the happy memories we have of the other person. Death revives our hearts, first by wounding them, and then by showing us that our memories of those who have passed are often quite loving, even if our relationship with them was also punctuated with pain. Our friends and family members continue to live in the forms of stories that we tell. When we retell the stories of our deceased loved ones, we bequeath something that might otherwise have been lost forever. Our beloveds, having been shared through narrative and memory, now live on a bit longer in the minds of others. In this way, death teaches yet another important lesson about life and the resilience of the human spirit.

Resilience is the capacity to pick yourself up again, to reopen yourself to the possibility of the present, to do this deep dive into your inner world, to bear the burdens that life heaps on you, and still remain in contact with this reservoir of love inside of you. It is the capacity to bear all of it and still remain compassionate rather than having your heart shutter itself with bitterness. It is the capacity to face death—the loss of others, the death of the ego—time and again and still feel reverence in the face of life's unfolding. I cannot say that I've mastered it. Perhaps—like my great-grandmother—I, too, will reach a point where my heart has been split one time too many, and I will be ready to say goodbye.

Helping others through death or facing immense grief doesn't necessarily prepare you to deal with your own death. Facing your fear of your own mortality is a critical step on the spiritual path. It is no easy task to get in touch with your own fear of death. Most times, even when you think you've faced your fear, you haven't.

When I was on ayahuasca, the very first night, the plant medicine took away my family—my husband and our two cats. It was incredibly painful to have my family taken from me. But I have a special bond with one of our two cats, Lily. For some reason we have connected in a way I really never thought possible. We spend a lot of time together; she sits on my lap in ways that she doesn't with my husband (who has an equally strong bond with our other cat, Charlie), and I often ponder how I will handle the moment that Lily dies. During the plant medicine ceremony, after I was already sobbing at the loss of Max and Charlie, the ayahuasca took Lily away, and it nearly broke me. I remember wailing, "I'm not ready for this." I'm still not, for all that I practice living without attachment.

One step is to begin to notice the ways you keep death at bay around you. Sometimes people do not want to think about power of attorney, wills, or burial plots. Those formalities are now further complicated by the decisions we must make with our digital lives, with Facebook settings to describe what happens to our content after we've died. New social norms are still emerging, like whether it's acceptable to "unfriend" someone who has passed whose account was never closed.

Do you turn off the news whenever death or tragedy is brought up? Do you avoid the obituary section of the newspaper? It can be an incredibly powerful practice to write your own obituary. How would you want it read? What would you want to hear others say at a memorial service? Are your current actions leading them to make those remarks or do you recognize that, if people were bluntly honest, your memorial might not seem so charitable?

If I want to connect to my sense of life and death, I might

begin with the simplest practice, so ubiquitous that often it is lost upon us until we struggle to do it: breathe. When I was younger, I had asthma, and nothing makes clearer the line between life and death than gasping for air.

I sometimes wondered why God had given me asthma. Why make life difficult in this way? But I learned a kind of tenderness around my breath that made it feel so much more precious to me. My asthma later faded, but my lungs have always remained a bit sensitive to cold—a gentle reminder that life and death are found in the rise and fall of the chest. When I watch my body breathing, as in meditation, I am witnessing a microcosm of life and death. That first inhalation as a newborn was the moment that I signaled to the world that I was here to stay by taking a small piece of the world into me. And I know that I will signal that my time here is over when I send my last breath back to the world, as if a silent goodbye. Until then, it helps me to watch my breath with that reverence. Whether you call it life, God, the divine, or Spirit—some invisible force moves my breath for me. Then I can marvel at the simplicity and grace of it moving through me, one breath at a time.

This simple shift reminds me that I am not separate from the world, but that I take it in with each inhalation, and return a part of me to it with each exhalation. My oneness with the world begins with the breath. Where do I begin, and where does the world end? I can't find that line in my breath. The boundary gets lost in vapor.

I can then bring this reverence to the bodies of everyone I encounter, setting aside differences to see that, however mundane it might sound, the divine spirit breathes for them too. How simple is it to be reminded that the breath moves through each and every one of us? How much can I be in awe of that majestic movement between each of us and the world? Nothing is more humbling to me than to ask: Who am I to judge where God has chosen to place Its breath? I cannot. I can only be grateful for this breath. And for yours. And this next one, not knowing when the divine will decide that it is the moment to return my breath—or yours—to the air for the last time.

* * *

You can also meditate directly on your own death. This can be a very challenging practice. It begins by imagining your funeral or memorial service. What people have shown up to mourn your passing? What remarks do they offer? What expressions do they have on their faces? Allow yourself to imagine this with rich texture so that you might get in touch with your fear of death. How did you die? This is a very triggering question that might invite a lot of fear to the surface very quickly. You might even have a deep fear of dying in a particular manner. My very worst fear of death is being trapped somewhere, where I would eventually run out of oxygen, or wouldn't be able to eat or drink and would eventually perish for lack of nourishment. The key aspects are being alone, being claustrophobic, and being deprived. Being trapped in some kind of underground tunnel, unable to move, unable to reach for help, left to die from lack of oxygen or malnourishment feels to me like the most soul-crushing means of departing this world.

This exercise is not meant to inspire depression, but to remind you of physical reality so that you can then renew your passion for life. How many of us have felt some kind of illness, a cough, a pain, a random jolt, and have flashed ever so quickly on the thought that this might be the end? Or we've been in an accident, suffered a massive injury, or maybe very nearly missed one, and we are reminded how it feels when death is close. When we get in touch with our fear around death and how much we have kept it at bay, we can use that energy to develop a sense of urgency. Recalling these moments can infuse us with the sense of how precious our time is and remind us not to fritter our lives away on activities that don't truly matter to us. That is not a call to say that you should spend your time in hedonistic pleasure at the expense of everyone and everything else. But if your soul longs, even aches, for something else, you must honor that before your time runs out. It might even require massive change to separate yourself from circumstances you've long accepted that do not reflect the truth of who you are. Those are moments to regather the sense of preciousness of our time here that is indeed limited, and to make the most of it.

Will you, at the end of your life, be able to look at yourself and say that you gave all you had to give? That is the question I ask myself when I want to invoke my future death as a way to motivate my present self. Some might ask what others will think of you, but that sense of approval is not what drives me— and while it would be rewarding to hear that others thought of me as compassionate, or as having an impact on their lives— ultimately, I must be at peace with what I have contributed to this world. I ask myself this question, not with a sense of lack or judgment or duty, but with a sense of having allowed myself to be fully myself. Is there more of me to give, to express, to unfold? That may not be the question that motivates you. That is part of your path, to go within and find the question that allows death to speak to you in a way that actually inspires you rather than filling you with dread.

THE DEATH OF OUR DREAMS

Even when we hold onto the preciousness of our time here and use it wisely, we will ultimately never accomplish everything we might have. One of the reasons we often do not want to think about death is that we begin to evaluate our lives, asking if we have fulfilled our goals or realized ourselves in the way that we had hoped to. We start to compare what we've done against some checklist of accomplishments or how much we feel we've fulfilled the mission of our soul. We start to feel more keenly the gap between who we are now and the ideal we have for ourselves. Sometimes we might even get mired in regret.

Part of reconciling ourselves with the truth of our eventual demise is that we have to accept that our vision for our lives shifts as we get older. Before physical death, we have to face the death of certain parts of our lives, the dreams we may have wanted to pursue and never did; the dreams we did pursue and failed to achieve. Death infuses our lives, not just in the loss of loved ones and the promise of our eventual perishing, but in the ways that chapters of our lives close as the years pass.

When we are young, we often have ambitious dreams and big plans for the future. We all start out hoping that one day we'll be someone who makes a mark on the world—someone who creates great art or writing or music or a new invention, or someone who becomes a leader, a healer, a teacher, or a guide who helps others. We all have aspirations. Over time, the ebbs and flows of life push and prod us. We get hurt and nurse our wounds. We get distracted and find ourselves off course. We get scared and backtrack. We find new courage and forge ahead. In our heart of hearts, we know that we are powerful, creative, and divinely inspired. We know that we have gifts to share.

But the simple reality is that along the way, with the passage of time, we end up letting go of certain dreams or possibilities. We recognize that options are no longer available to us. There is a reality that we cannot always be everything. I will never be a gymnast, an astronaut, or a Grammy-Award-winning singer. These are simple truths. My body is too old to do backflips or handle the stresses of being lifted out of our planet's orbit, and I cannot carry a tune. Should I lament these truths or find freedom in the fact that these are avenues I know not to pursue? Our bodies can no longer sustain certain activities, or we accept that they never could. We make choices and let go of options, relegating them to the path not taken.

At some point, your world—or at least the opportunities you see—starts to shrink. You might not become the film star or the sports figure or the renowned artist or the successful entrepreneur or the wild inventor or the political maverick or the social media influencer or the wellness guru or the person whose name everybody knows. For some of us, we have tried again and again, and success has eluded us, forcing us to look at other possibilities.

The reality is that you get a bit older and a little more tired, and the seeds of doubt you've tried not to water remain there, buried in the soil of your psyche, holding onto just enough life that when your tears flow from another disappointment, those seeds start to grow. Responsibilities, demands, and other tasks lay claim to your time. Perhaps you have children or parents whose care requires your attention and sacrifice. Perhaps you realize that the dreams you've been pursuing were never yours, and you don't know what your true dreams are. These are the moments when we take stock of our lives and ask why we are here.

This is part of what the spiritual path demands: You accept these forms of death as part of the fabric of our lives. This is where surrender and death unite. We don't often acknowledge this way that death shapes our journey. You tell yourself that your life now is good enough. You continue to work, create, and put yourself out there. At some point, a certain kind of success seems to be beyond your reach, and others—younger, faster, fresher, and hungrier—start to climb ahead of you. Your world shrinks a little bit more. The revised dream gets revised again, maybe a little smaller, a little less ambitious. Or a lot smaller, a lot less ambitious, depending on what life has sent your way. Or you just stop looking for your life's purpose, giving up on having a dream at all.

At a certain point, we begin to take stock, realizing that our time here is finite. You might put the dreams aside, however tiny they've become, thinking they're no longer possible or realistic, or you might continue to march on. Some might find that the dream blooms, out of nowhere, after decades of effort, blossoming into something wonderful. Others continue to carve out their place in the world, making peace with what that finally looks like.

Hopefully, along the way, we stop to look beyond our dreams at the friends we've made, the people we've loved, and the homes we've built. We might look at the lives we've touched, and who has touched us along the way. We might take stock and feel appreciation for good health, material comforts, or big adventures. Death, in taking away options, often reminds us to look at all that we have managed to do along the way. We might recall with sweet fondness the times we helped out others, held someone's hand, or listened. And in that moment, we might pause and see our lives a bit differently. You surrender to the life you have, rather than mourning the life you didn't lead.

One of my dreams that I eventually had to release was having a child. Life did not present me with the opportunity to have kids. I grew up at a time when gay couples did not regularly adopt, and I ended up marrying someone who, like me, did not feel strongly about having children. But at moments, I've been hit with a pang of melancholy, a sense that I had lost the kind of love and connection that can only happen between a parent and a child. I will never know that form of love. Accepting that loss as a possibility unfulfilled, a path not taken, is a way of accepting a certain kind of death. Doing so allowed me to feel gratitude for what I do have in my life and to focus on the possibilities that not having a child has afforded me. Mourning the loss of one possibility opened me to the presence of a possibility that the first one would have prevented me from experiencing. In this way, death showed me to honor and be grateful for the life that I have chosen for myself.

It is not with melancholy that I see parts of myself dying off and being stripped away as I get older and closer to death. This is part of the integration of the wisdom around identity, resurrection, and death as integral parts of life. Instead, I can marvel at the way my life has unfolded with incredible grace, that my body might return to the earth and become grass or trees, nourishing life in a new way, and that my spirit might move on, preparing for another journey. I like to imagine that my life in this incarnation, as a person named Patrick, will be a future self's past life, for him or her to uncover at some point. Doing so reminds me to tread lightly, to leave a faint footstep in this realm, to forgive and love easily and often, so that I can lessen the burden that my soul's future life will have to resolve.

* * *

There are moments when writing itself feels like the entire process of life and death—a birth and an ending. More than any other chapter in this book, I have struggled to come to a conclusion about death that feels satisfying. What wisdom do I have to impart to you beyond the words already expressed? After all, to paraphrase the Zen priest, I have not experienced death myself. I confess that I still hold fast to the hope that when I die, I will find myself greeted by my father, my great-grandmother, Sally, my cats, and everybody else I've loved who passed before me. I would be lying if I said I didn't harbor the belief that there is a future for my consciousness with the memories of my life here. I know that my soul is eternal, but what about my consciousness? They are not necessarily the same.

The belief in our eternal spirit, in the timelessness of the soul, which moves on from our physical form to return to the source of life, is hardly new or novel. My experiences in consciousness and energy have taught me that the life energy that moves through me and is my connection to God will never cease. My own guidance from the divine tells me that life continues afterwards. I could even appeal to the principle of physics that energy never ends but is only transformed. But I cannot speak with any kind of experience in a way that would confirm what it is like to live outside a body. I do not know what it is like to be conscious without physical form. We might like to imagine ourselves as ghosts, as somehow maintaining the physical shape of our current forms but transparent and able to pass through walls. Or perhaps we are invisible, watching from afar. These are all creative expressions of what might be, but they are also a distraction from the here and now, from what it means to live with exquisite awareness that we are always in the shadow of death.

Still, the thought of reuniting with my loved ones who have passed gives me some kind of comfort. The same is true of my deep connection to the divine that I feel flowing through my body and my breath. Life and death are intertwined with each passing moment. To embrace one is to embrace the other. As Kahlil Gibran says in *The Prophet*, "You would know the secret of death. But how shall you find it unless you seek it in the heart of life?"[1] Death has not yet come for me. With gratitude and reverence, I turn to life, to my husband and our two cats, to enjoy the rest of this day. After all, it could be my last.

CONCLUSION:
YOU ARE PARADOX EMBODIED

⫴

Until the moment of our death, time plays an indispensable yet mysterious role in our lives. As we have seen throughout this book, we think of time as linear, but in fact, each of us must navigate our psychological relationship to time along with an inexorable march toward death. In that way, there are as many timelines as there are individuals in the world. All of us travel back in time through our memories, leap to the future with excitement or worry, and experience the present through the lens of our consciousness. Time feels constitutive, essential to our lives, yet it bends and warps beneath the weight of our willingness to pay attention to it. Time seems both fixed and fluid all at once.

The German television series, *Dark*, plunders these paradoxical aspects of time to great effect. The story begins in 2019 with a boy named Mickel, who passes through a portal that takes him back to 1986, before he was born. He remains stuck in that early time period, meeting his future parents when they were teenagers. As he grows older, he is still trapped in the past when his mother gives birth to him in 1992. He therefore exists as two versions, of different ages, in the same place. From there, a whole host of other illogical outcomes of time travel ensue, including the mindboggling twist of a daughter who, by traveling back in time, turns out to be her own mother.

Another one of the major paradoxes in time revolves around the origin of a book, *A Journey Through Time*, which provides instructions for how to build a time machine. One of the protagonists uses the time machine laid out in the book to take the book back in time to its author, before he has written it. When the protagonist gives him a copy, the author then copies his own book and publishes it. Would he have written it without the future protagonist coming back in time to give it to him?

The answer is unclear. The book's creation no longer has a starting point. The author of the book was only able to write it because a future copy was given to him. A future object, supposedly created in the past, is brought back to the past, where its arrival at that time becomes the origin for its creation. The book has no original point of creation, yet it exists. It is part of a loop. The same is true of the daughter who becomes her own mother. This is known as the bootstrap paradox. We depend on time's linearity for our understanding of creation. Without it, we get lost in circularity.

As fascinating as it is to ponder the paradoxes of time travel, we need not turn to science fiction to see that the paradoxical nature of time shapes our very reality. In *The Elegant Universe*, Brian Greene explains that paradox is a basic, if revolutionary, premise about the nature of reality.

Greene describes a hypothetical experiment in which two presidents of embattled nations are each at the end of a long train traveling at high speed.[1] They have agreed to sign a peace treaty simultaneously, when a light bulb situated in the middle of the train is turned on. One of those heads of state is at the front of the train, facing the back; the other is at the back of the train, facing the front. The light travels from the center to the front and the back of the train, triggering the heads of state to sign their copy of the treaty.

This is where time's paradox begins. According to Greene, those on the train witnessing this event all agree that each person signed the treaty at the same time. Yet those watching at a distance from a nonmoving platform, and thus stationary in relation to the fast-moving train, perceive that one of them signed the document just slightly earlier than the other—the light reached the president at the back of the train, facing the front, just fractions of a second earlier. For the passengers on the train, the distance between the two heads of state remained equal. For the viewers on a fixed platform, the president who was traveling in the same direction as the train "caught up to" the light faster because, from their vantage point, he was moving toward the light bulb, and thus the light had to travel less distance to reach him, while the other head of state was traveling away from the light.

The discrepancy in views between the moving observers and those stationary ones on the platform is explained by the theory of special relativity. Greene explains that a set of observers moving at a certain rate of motion will agree on one perspective, while another group moving at a different rate of motion will have another perspective, and "both are right . . . each perspective has an equal claim on truth. The only subtlety here is that the respective truths seem to be contradictory." When it comes to time, two different perspectives, although mutually exclusive, can hold equal claims to truth.[2]

Just as Einstein's insights into relativity point to competing yet equally true perspectives, in a similar way, spirituality asks you to hold two mutually exclusive perspectives simultaneously. This has been the fundamental message of this book.

This is a very different perspective from our conventional way of looking at the world, which often seeks some kind of coherence, consistency, and finality for its answers. The spiritual principles that have occupied these pages often turned on a tension between two opposing views that were not meant to be resolved by choosing one over the other. In this way, spirituality resembles something like the perennial divide between quantum physics, with its focus on ever smaller subatomic particles, and general relativity, with its focus on much larger objects: Each theory suffices to explain its domain, but they are internally inconsistent with each other.[3] Each one has a verifiable claim to truth, yet they are mutually exclusive absent some other organizing principle. So, too, spirituality asks you to hold a series of principles without resolving their contradictions and ignoring the discomfort that holding both might inspire in you.

COMPETING CLAIMS TO TRUTH

This book has explored a series of contradictions: You are energy, yet you are also matter. You are one with all, yet you are also a sovereign being with a material body that is separate from others. You are filled with emotional energy, yet your essence is love. You are perfect just as you are, yet you are also in need of profound healing. You exist only in the present moment, yet our psychic lives are tied invariably to the past and a future. In that future you will die physically, yet your spirit is eternal. Each is true, yet if you hold only one and dispense with the other, you are left with an incomplete picture.

Time is the principal source of paradox for human life. To reflect on life from a spiritual perspective means that we have to grapple with death. We have to accept that we all age and that our physical bodies will perish. In short, our clock time on this planet is limited. Yet spirituality also reminds us that the only moment of time that we experience is the present moment. We can never return to the past or jump to the future: Our reflections of the past and fantasies about the future are our mental projections taking place in the present moment. Spirituality asks us to relate to life as though time were finite *and* as if linear time did not exist, to acknowledge that life is one present moment after another. We cannot escape the passage of time, and yet we only exist in a single moment. We add to this the additional layer that our spirit is eternal, that it is beyond time. We experience this state when we fall out of time through meditation or our crown chakras open and our consciousness connects with the divine. In this way, time ends, time never ends, time always flows forward, and time exists only as a single moment. All of these perceptions of time have claims to truth.

The path of wisdom often leads to some kind of internal contradiction where logic and linearity wind back around, leaving you with competing propositions about the nature of life and the soul. Paradox and contradiction are essential to spiritual wisdom. Uncertainty and doubt, not knowing, and holding mutually exclusive positions are a key part of the spiritual path, of moving beyond the rational mind's effort to navigate the world. We embrace paradox by accepting mutually exclusive principles without resolving their conflict. Living at the intersection of paradox is where we find what it means to be both divine and human at the same time.

In embracing what seem like mutually exclusive truths, you overturn your conventional perception of time and space. When we turn to that most essential dimension of human life—your emotions—we see how our pain anchors us to the past, yet that pain is also a portal to your highest self. You only find the divine by diving into darkness; you don't find the sublime by searching outward. Going inward, paradoxically, doesn't lead to solipsism but expansion. Going inward leads to clearing out the pain, opening yourself up to more light—the light of your own compassion for your pain. In this way, the pain becomes a gift, a map to the treasure of your true self, the reservoir of unconditional love within you, hidden on the other side of that pain. The very source of our discontent, it turns out, is the path to our healing. What we saw as a wound ends up being a pathway to wisdom.

But that path of going inward is also a going backward, through your memories of prior pain to discover your own capacity to be present to that which you have carried with you, moment after moment. You learn along the way that your body carries with it sensations and a capacity to remember. Buried deep in its folds are pockets of unresolved pain. Trauma winds its tendrils through the skin and bones, not just the mind. Your body, then, is not just matter—it is also energy. Triggered in the present, our bodies erupt, flush with embarrassment, shame, sadness, anger, or some other feeling pouring into us. Whatever we experience in the present gets added as a new layer of existential sediment. The emotional energy of the moment is transcribed into tissue.

In this way, we are houses of wave and particle, energy and matter, and we build ourselves, layer after layer, out of memory and cognition to form a self with an identity. We lay claim to a certain kind of being only to realize that such a claim does nothing to create solidity or permanence. Our identities are these amalgams of seemingly fixed patterns that fluctuate as fluid experimentations with labels. This conventional understanding of the self actually takes us away from a sense of coherence. We are fragmented, incoherent, and constantly changing. Our claims to identity also mean that we perceive the present in light of the past, where we have already faced so much fear, and the fearful shadow of our future death, which makes the present almost inaccessible. Our sense of identity suggests a core self, something authentic and solid, but when you peel back the layers you realize that it is an illusion crafted in language, memory, and feeling.

Paradoxically, it is only by letting go of the self that you find true permanence. When you release your perception of separation, the power of awareness and presence becomes so much more solid than the fragile ego could ever foster. In that way, the power of our memory and language is also the path of liberation. It is not a prison to which we are condemned. We use time to identify a story. The house we've built for ourselves out of words can be dismantled and rebuilt. We can rewrite that story by going back over our past and forgiving the people who've caused us pain and helped shape our lives in ways that are not affirming. By doing so, we create a new relationship to the present moment. This is the practice of resurrection. Just as each second is a new moment of time—so, too, can we use that temporality to birth ourselves a new sense of self.

Time is malleable, and yet also inescapable, as we will all die. The paradox of embracing death is not that we seek to die but accepting our inevitable death opens us up to the depth of life itself. If we avoid death, allowing our fear to run our lives, we never quite touch life itself. Death is, it turns out, life giving. The fear of death is one that invites much speculation about whether we are eternal, whether our soul or consciousness goes on. I certainly have that belief, but it in no way eliminates the reality that my body will age and eventually cease to function. In this way, my body is bound by time even if my soul is not.

Perhaps no paradox in spirituality is more powerful than the tension between oneness and sovereignty. We all conceive of ourselves as if we were entirely separate from each other. We inhabit separate bodies with separate minds, each of us a discrete, unique human being. This is the source of our emotional strife, our fear of death, and our penchant for judgment. It is the source of the pain and suffering that permeates our world. At the same time, none of us exists separately. We were brought into this world through another human being, our mother, and our lives have depended fundamentally on our connections to each other. We are never really separate at all, just occupying time and space in different ways, each of us living together, sometimes in unison, sometimes in conflict. We have always depended for our survival on the loving presence of others who have tended to our needs. No one is truly alone, for even if you've managed to isolate yourself, grow your own food, provide for your own energy, you did so by virtue of legal agreements with many others that allowed you to purchase your land and hold title to it, to benefit from the laws that prevent trespass, etc. We are in constant contact with the rest of the world. And we should revel in the freedom that such contact affords. Yet we each need to exercise the power of our choice over our lives, and we must value our right to exercise control over our own bodies.

We therefore must accept our autonomous, independent forms, and at the same time, acknowledge that such independence and autonomy is an illusion. Spirituality asks us to hold each of these positions as equally valid and precious: We are each unique beings, with unique lives, desiring to express the truth of who we are, however we might define that truth for ourselves; and at the same time, we are never separate or disconnected, even when we appear to be in isolation. We only exist in and through each other—working collectively to feed and nourish our physical bodies and by forming families, friendships, communities, and societies.

The principles of oneness and sovereignty allow us to embrace sameness and diversity all at once. We are all different, with different identities, preferences, languages, histories, hopes, and dreams. Yet we are all the same in that we all share the same core issues and desires of wanting to belong and feel loved, to believe that we are worthy, and to feel that we can be our true selves. We occupy different bodies, with unique faces and identities, but we all share the desire to become the fullest expression of who we believe ourselves to be. We all want to know our purpose and feel that we matter. We all share this inherent connection to life, but we all develop that relationship differently, according to the dictates of the soul and the choices we make.

TRANSCENDENCE REQUIRES DUALITY

As we have seen, it is quite common among spiritual seekers to attempt to resolve these paradoxes by abandoning one position for another. For example, in an effort to grapple with the body's pain and temporal limits, people often want to reject the body and lay claim to being light. You'll find many spiritual people who will tell you that you are not a body, that it is an illusion. Or, in the face of individuality that seems messy, filled with emotion and desire, and prone to interpersonal conflict, a spiritual seeker will lay claim to the view that we are all one, and that you are everybody, and they are you.

Instead of embracing paradox, a seeker can attempt to resolve it by seeing these as two distinct realms or dimensions. You accomplish this feat by treating the first set of principles as relative truth, or duality, and the second set of principles as universal truth, or transcendence, and positing that your goal is to move from relative to universal truth. In my view, this is an attempted shortcut to mastery that eliminates the relative in favor of the universal. It pits paradox and duality against transcendence. Disavowing the body and emphasizing that you are light, saying there is no time and we are eternal, or proclaiming oneness and interdependence without acknowledging separation—these are all ways of avoiding the messy reality of life in a physical body on the planet. If you focus on being energy at the expense of matter, or if you embrace the present and ignore the passage of time, you cut yourself off from other dimensions of reality.

The risk is that the ego falls prey to the temptation of bypass so as to avoid the complexities that these competing truths create for our lived, embodied experiences here on this planet. Treating the universal as the goal becomes a means to escape and bypass the relative world in which we all start and where most people remain their entire lives. When spiritual seekers pursue transcendence to avoid duality, they end up cutting themselves off from the rest of the world, hoping to remain forever in the bliss and never experience negativity or conflict. That's different from saying that they actively choose their lives and do not foster judgment, criticism, or emotional pain. Or that they want to ignore the truth of their bodies, treating their sexuality as a sinful desire to be eradicated. This approach to spirituality becomes a way to avoid the uncomfortable work of dealing with our thoughts and emotions, resolving interpersonal conflict, and living in what can often seem like a deeply cruel world.

There is another way of resolving this tension, which is to acknowledge that we do not properly understand each of these principles, and that there is another perspective that allows us to hold them all simultaneously. If we see them as a dialectic, where one allows the other to exist, without which neither would exist, then we can understand what it means to hold them both. Dialectical thinking is not meant to resolve the contradiction but embrace it by seeing how both positions depend on, not exclude, the other. Transcendence, or enlightenment, means moving beyond duality, but it does not mean leaving duality behind altogether. Rather, transcendence comes from duality, and oneness comes from separation. These are not socially constructed binary oppositions, like Democrats vs. Republicans, which are crude means by which our egos simplify the world. Dialectical concepts are the basic components that give rise to reality.

One way to enter dialectical thinking is by exploring briefly one of the great paradoxes of spirituality—that of free will. I had an encounter with plant medicine that showed me how free will is not what we understand it to be. In the darkness of the ceremonial room deep in the Amazon, the ayahuasca spoke to me and said, "There is no free will. It is the will of the Mother." But as I heard this sentence in my mind, I understood that it was not that we lacked free will, in the sense that our lives were determined from the outset, and we could not make choices, as if we were destined for a single fate. Rather, her meaning was that there are no wrong choices because all of our choices are already part of the will of the divine. Imagine that our lives had an infinite number of paths, all of them part of our life plan. Think of it as fate with infinite destinations. Your life is sort of a choose-your-own-adventure book, with infinite options. Countless choices are available to you—that we have choice at all is part of divine will.

Mother Nature's message, conveyed through the ayahuasca,

is that we should relinquish the fear we have of exercising our power, because the power to choose, at each and every moment, is our divine power. We are exercising divine will when we exercise personal choice. When coupled with trust and surrender, it means that no choice is ever wrong—every choice will lead us to something we are meant to learn. Choice forces us to relinquish the idea that our life's blueprint is designed to lead us to fulfill a single mission in one particular way. That is the way humans typically think. The vision that the divine has for our lives is infinitely richer and more complex.

The resolution, then, of the paradox of these spiritual principles about life is not to try to prove one is right and the other wrong. It is to see that our understanding of them as exclusive is incomplete, and there is another perspective that allows us to hold them together. In so doing, the power of paradox is that it moves you beyond the logical dictates of the reasoning mind to experience something that the mind, in relinquishing its normal efforts to process, normally cannot.

This is similar to the mental exercise of koan practice in the Zen tradition. Koans are short and simple puzzles that are designed to lead the Zen student out of the conceptual mind that is attached to certain concepts and ways of thinking; koan practice is designed to short-circuit the normal avenues of thought. Many of you are probably familiar with one of the most famous of them: What is the sound of one hand clapping? The answer is not found by identifying a particular frequency or someone unmasking a recording and definitively pinning down the sound of one hand clapping.

The power and purpose of the koan is the way that its question takes your mind down certain well-traveled rational paths, poses more questions, and leads it to its own conceptual limitations. The koan disturbs the kinds of outcomes and answers the mind seeks. It leads the mind to a place of thought, and then a collapse of thinking, and another effort at answering. As you grapple with the koan, you see the machinery of your mind in action, breaking down words, posing counterarguments, or even searching for a philosophical answer that makes you feel clever. The koan takes you to a place where the mind normally does not travel.

Koans are not the only practice that can shake up your mind. Life took me on a very different journey than most, to a kundalini awakening and a discovery of the vast repository of energy that each of us is made of. My rational mind had to accommodate my experience, which began with receiving beautiful loving energy from teachers and healers, and then experiencing this energy erupt within myself. What seemed like it was coming from the outside was already inside. In all of these experiences, I have learned that my perception of what it means to be human had to shift, and what I thought of as matter was also energy. What I thought of as outside, was inside; these physical distinctions were collapsing. Then I would come back into my body and interact with the world as before. Space and time had returned to "normal." This was a profound letting go of my normal concepts for perceiving reality.

The bliss that comes from the self as it dissolves into the divine is immeasurable and indescribable. Aside from the kundalini awakening, which by far is the greatest spiritual experience of my life, I've had other moments of such ego dissolution. On one occasion, I was walking through my neighborhood, and the thought flashed through me: *Where is Patrick?* And the answer came as swiftly: *Nowhere and everywhere.* Suddenly, my mind let go of any attempt at holding onto a coherent sense of self, and I felt what it was like to be just a series of reactions—what the Buddhists call "causes and conditions"—without any core sense of being. I felt the loosening as my ego temporarily dissolved into nothing more than a host of causes and effects. There was no "core" me at that moment. I felt the utter simplicity of it all and fell to a fit of laughter on the street. Then my ego resumed, reorienting itself in time and space, and my normal sense of self returned.

I understand why the allure of transcendence, of somehow escaping the material, conventional world, is so great for so many spiritual seekers. There is incredible bliss, peace, and love to be found in experiencing that kind of divine union. Whether we call it enlightenment or transcendence or ascension—if that's what we mean by these kinds of ego-dissolving experiences—the fact is that bliss is not a place from which you can live. You can't remain there. The veil is pulled back so you can peek inside the matrix, and the curtain is drawn again.

And there's nothing wrong with that, because we are meant to experience both planes. The illusion is not that we have a self. The illusion is that the sense of self that we have is all there is. We have a self because we create one. But it's the creation of something that pretends to be all there is, the whole truth of who we are. We are also not a self, and experiencing that dissolution is, as I said, quite blissful. But that doesn't mean that you're supposed to leave behind the self forever, or that somehow not living every moment in the bliss of selflessness is a failure. It's not. Rather, we experience the wonder and bliss from selflessness by returning to self, and leaving again, coming back into bliss, and then back into a self.

Think of yourself as an infinity symbol, separating into two strands that unite as one, and then separating again into two, over and again. You are the drop of water that becomes part of the ocean, only to then migrate into moisture as part of a cloud and fall back into the ocean as a drop of rain, cycling through oneness and separation in a never-ending process. Enlightenment is not occupying one state at the expense of the other. It is the paradox that these seemingly mutually exclusive states require each other, to hold both as true at the same time even though one seemingly negates the other. Enlightenment, then, is your capacity to live in the paradox by believing simultaneously two truths, one relative, the other universal, without resolving their supposed incompatibility.

Our ability to live with paradox requires that we depart from our conventional ways of thinking—our typical, linear, rational discourses—even as we depend on them (and this entire volume does). Indeed, this very argument depends on a rational mind, and much of the preceding work in this book has been focused on unraveling the assumptions we make by leading you logically to see where our conventional wisdom belies its own truth. Logic is not abandoned but taken to its conceptual limit. When we break down our conceptual understanding, we see that our language creates the world we perceive, our minds construct space and time, and when we can pierce that construction, we can experience the bliss of formlessness.

We then return to form, seeing the same world we saw before, but it's not quite the same, like me becoming one with the landscape outside the train described in Chapter 3. In some way, it is more magical, for we can learn to perceive the world, and all the people in it, as illuminated from within by the energy or light that is the essence beyond form. We have this ability to perceive the light, or the divine, in everyone and everything when we release ourselves from the bind of seeing these principles as contradictory, of seeing the need to resolve them in a way that satisfies our rational or scientific minds. Doing so takes us out of the realm of a kind of intellectual certainty into the realm of a mystical space. Life starts to look like a riddle that need not be unraveled, for we can just rest in the mystery, in that space where the mind has no answer and no longer searches for one. Mystery is scary only to the rational mind, which sees hidden danger. To the awakened mind, seeing the world through the eyes of the divine, mystery is magical.

This is a point that is often missed in the vogue of "ascension" as the replacement paradigm for enlightenment. Our vocabulary continues to betray our allegiance to certain basic concepts like some kind of progress that takes us higher (and therefore "better") from a "lower" (and therefore "worse") state of consciousness. There, the emphasis is on reaching a certain kind of vibrational state, a level of frequency. What sometimes gets lost is the perception that this means that you leave behind the material world. In fact, what it means is that you leave behind the normal, conventional ways of relating to the material world. The point is not to "ascend" or "transcend" and leave behind the body. Rather, it is to see our material world, including its deeply entrenched consciousness of duality, from a new perspective. If you reject it, you've installed once again a hierarchy and a linear trajectory. You see one as beneath the other. This is where spiritual bypass and judgment have sneaked into the party through the back door. For when you come back to duality after being in transcendence, you start to see that the relative world—the world of the body, of linear time, of death, of messy emotions—is just as spectacular as the transcendent state of feeling united with the divine.

Because in truth, there is no difference. It is the construction of the mind that sees, and thus experiences, the relative world and the divine as different from each other. Therein lies the magic: Once you've truly connected with the divine inside, which once seemed outside of you, all the parts that seem like they're at odds with a spiritual life no longer are. I love being in a mortal aging body, filled with emotions and connecting and disconnecting and reconnecting with others. Each time you find yourself reacting to the material world in hopes of being elsewhere, in some transcendent plane, that is where your work lies. You've just reached a new portal, another dimension through which to step. You hold both duality and transcendence with equal reverence because they are not false binaries. Rather, they are each in dialectical tension, in which one gives rise to the other. All of them are versions of divine energy, taking shape, dissolving into formlessness, and then taking a new shape.

There is tremendous freedom in this view of spirituality. Rather than feeling unfairly bound to our earthly existence, our material reality becomes a source of joy. Within the constraint of being bound by duality, we find the freedom to explore transcendence. Being in duality starts to feel transcendent. Freedom comes not from escaping the self, but from escaping the illusion that the created, conditioned self is all there is. This is the freedom that allows for the self to be created and recreated anew, from moment to moment. Freedom is found in this capacity to see the self as a portal to the infinite. Freedom is found in our capacity to resurrect ourselves, from moment to moment, where one moment can be blissful and the next moment, painful. So much wonder and joy come from occupying a self who might dissolve into divine union and then return again to form. Isn't that the cycle of life and death itself? Accept that you can be merged with God and at the same time be a human being with an ego walking around in time and space, interacting with other humans. You are both, at the same time. You are the riddle that cannot be resolved. You are a walking koan. You are the infinity symbol.

For when we hold duality and transcendence, the relative

and the universal, together, we step into a place where our rigid sense of self finally fades. This blurring of the lines between you and the rest of the world is the undoing of separation, not just between you and the divine, but between you and *everything*. Living at the intersection of paradox means upending your conventional way of constructing the world through separation, namely, viewing everything as either inside and outside, you and me, where my sense of self in time and space is a rigid rather than fluid border. You find your true self by letting go of who you (think you) are, only to discover that there is no self.

From that vantage point you understand your true self, which is a version of identity very different from what you experience now, with its borders and boundaries and rules and expectations and beliefs about yourself and others. To get there, you have to release a story you may have told yourself for many years, only to realize that the parts of you that were so painful are now the pathways to this buried self. But once you release your story about your pain, you realize that you're never done healing, and you're never whole. Once you accept that healing never ends, you realize that emotions are not signs of being broken or unhealed, and then you're whole again. From that new perspective, you can continue to resolve your pain. Pain is that sensation that you felt when you believed, erroneously, that you were less than your divine self. Pain is what allows you to come back to knowing what the divine self feels like. After all, if you had never felt pain, would you know what bliss feels like?

We accomplish this transcendence with duality by drawing closer to material reality, not escaping it, and we can draw closer to it by slowing down. We assume that if we were to slow down, we might miss out on doing all the things that we want to do; we wouldn't accomplish everything. It's as if we were all running around with bucket lists, frantically trying to cross off items before our time runs out. Our fear of our future death causes us to move swiftly; no time to waste, we might say. But, ironically, when we slow down, life becomes much fuller, not duller. Each second starts to take on a deeper resonance. It might seem, at first, like boredom. The mind is used to a certain kind of pace, with a certain kind of data. But when you slow down and take the time to be fully present to each and every moment, something kind of special emerges.

By way of example, in the 2021 film *The Map of Tiny Perfect Things*, the protagonists, two teenagers, a young man and a young woman, suddenly find themselves in a time loop in which the day starts over at midnight; no matter where they go or what they do, the world resets as soon as the clock strikes midnight. They soon learn that they have endless time to explore the world around them. By repeating the days over and over again, they slowly discover all of these wondrous moments, gone in the blink of an eye, that they had missed when they weren't paying attention.

They soon set as their mission to capture them all, each going around finding one such moment to share with the other—a hawk catching a fish out of the lake, a janitor momentarily playing a sublime tune on the piano, or a skateboarder executing a perfect jump. They soon develop a theory that when they've gathered and mapped all of the "perfect" moments, time will resume. After they map what they believe is all of those moments, the loop mysteriously does not end. It dawns on the woman that the reason they're still stuck is that there is one remaining piece: She has to accept that her mother is dying from cancer (which turned out to be the catalyst for this time loop) and let her go. Her mother tells her that even if she knew she would die of cancer, she wouldn't have changed anything about her life. The perfect moments are not always pleasurable.

Sometimes they are bittersweet. Avoiding pain doesn't prevent us from feeling pain but from living fully.

It's a simple message, but one we need reminding of again and again, as we get trapped in our own time loops of mundane activities, and time compresses and shrinks. We look back and think, time has passed so quickly. In truth, we never stopped to really take in the world around us. We moved through it by treating each moment like it was the same, when in fact each one is special. If we each slow down and watch with that kind of reverence and wonder for even the most seemingly trivial tasks, that's what we find. It's the reason Zen teaches us to find enlightenment in washing the dishes. There's an absolute magic in each second. It's as if the mystery of the world were daring us at each moment to peek a little more closely.

Along the way, we will fall back into separation. We will cycle through old patterns. Each of these moments is just another invitation to release our old ways of seeing the world. You might need to release the idea of growth and change. We are never static. Just as we might experience a certain level of equanimity, balance, bliss, or compassion, we are always still deepening our connection to all that is. We can take on emotional energy, or we might discover a pocket of pain that comes up for healing and release. The path is not linear, and we can revive old patterns of being, become a different version of who we are today that is not necessarily more positive or more loving. We still need to be vigilant for the ways that the ego attempts to bake our experiences into an identity it can hold onto.

You will come to see yourself as incoherent and inconsistent, and you will learn to find freedom in not limiting yourself or imposing on yourself some standard. As someone who values integrity, I bristle at inconsistency. But why not allow it in some ways? We are often internally at odds, and we splinter ourselves by trying to make sure all the pieces remain coherent. In this way, I must accept that I am inconsistent internally. Some days I am happy; others I am sad or prone to anger. I could pretend otherwise, and I know many meditators who mask their emotional fluctuations as signs of failure. But that's part of what needs to be released. We learn to let go of our linear mindset that says that once we've reached a certain level, we don't face demotion; once we've graduated, we don't have to repeat with a remedial lesson. Not so on the spiritual path. We might find ourselves realizing that to "win" at life, we must embrace "losing." If we want to grow or change in some way, we must accept ourselves just as we are right now. We start to realize that we fall back into binary thinking and judgment. At each moment, we fall out of alignment and heal. All it takes is a split second to recognize where you are resisting reality and to allow it once more. The heart constricts and then opens once again.

* * *

One of the greatest paradoxes and most beautiful lessons of life that I learned was what it meant to explore these very questions. For so long, I felt this deep calling to understand the nature of the self and our relationship to life. I always wondered, and at times worried, that it was an insular, solipsistic venture. But I couldn't help exploring questions of identity, self, and meaning, whether in literature, metaphysics, physics, spirituality, or law. I am constantly fascinated by the possibilities for understanding the self; the question of what it means to be human is an endless source of inspiration. My fascination was coupled with a deep reverence for and trust in life. When I am aligned with my soul, I feel this magic in the fabric of everything.

Why the world works as it does is still a mystery. Given all the possibilities for how energy and matter could take shape, isn't it a bit mindboggling that it takes this shape that we experience, and that in each second the universe doesn't implode? That alone, for me, is a source of wonder and awe, that each second actually exists as it does in this very second and still exists in the next. For isn't it possible that in the next second a cosmic failure might occur, provoking a quantum rupture? That it doesn't is part of the mystery and magic of the fabric of life itself. And part of why I can trust it.

All of my experiences in consciousness have impressed upon me the belief that our self has no core essence other than this cosmic energy that most closely resembles what we call love. It is when I bask in this reverence for life's never-ending possibilities that I recognize that writing about this search for myself has nothing whatsoever to do with me. The search only has meaning insofar as it allows me to be of service to others, to share insights that might allow others to find some piece of themselves, to be able to illuminate another's path—in whatever way I can. This work is ultimately not about me, but about you. It is only when I gave up the search for myself that I ended up finding myself after all. Isn't the paradox beautiful?

ACKNOWLEDGMENTS

⫘

First, I would like to thank Paul Cohen and Colin Rolfe for their tremendous work on this book.

I owe a huge debt to Lia Ottaviano for her editorial eye and advice on the original manuscript, which greatly improved its flow. Additional thanks to Dory Mayo for her careful edits, which polished the final version.

Profound thanks to the spiritual friends who have walked alongside me, sharing their love and support as we have pursued the calling of the soul. A deep bow of gratitude to the many teachers who have blessed me with their wisdom and insight, and to the seekers who have trusted me at times to guide them on their path. Unending gratitude and love for the divine itself, in all the forms and guises in which it has appeared and showered me with grace.

Finally, my greatest thanks go to my husband, Max, whose limitless love and support I cherish every day.

ABOUT THE AUTHOR

᠁

Patrick Paul Garlinger is an award-winning author who experienced a profound spiritual awakening over a decade ago when he began to meet numerous spiritual teachers and experience higher states of consciousness. He writes to help humanity transcend the way we think about the nature of reality and the meaning of life.

His first work, *When Thought Turns to Light*, is a primer on spiritual transformation that won the 2016 Living Now Spirit Award. That same year, his kundalini awakened, accelerating his spiritual evolution, and he downloaded a complete trilogy of channeled works. The first volume, *Seeds of Light: Channeled Transmissions on the Christ Consciousness*, was awarded the 2018 Living Now Silver Medal for Metaphysics. The second volume, *Bending Time: The Power to Live in the Now*, on how our consciousness is structured around time, was released in 2018. The third volume of the trilogy, *A World Without Identity: The Sacred Task of Uniting Humanity*, on the relationship between spirituality and social change, received the 2020 Living Now Silver Medal for World Peace.

Patrick lives in New York. For more information about his offerings, please visit www.patrickpaulgarlinger.com.

NOTES

INTRODUCTION

1   Out of profound respect and appreciation for those clients whose examples I have included to benefit the reader, I have altered key details and omitted any identifying information.

2   Some of the material in this book has been developed in prior works. Portions that previously appeared in article form have been substantially revised as part of the present volume.

CHAPTER 1

1   Itzhak Beery, *The Gift of Shamanism: Visionary Power, Ayahuasca Dreams, and Journeys to Other Realms* (Rochester, VT: Destiny Books, 2015), 58–59.

2   Kahlil Gibran, *The Prophet* (New York: Alfred A. Knopf, 1923), 52.

CHAPTER 2

1   Itzhak Beery, *The Gift of Shamanism: Visionary Power, Ayahuasca Dreams, and Journeys to Other Realms* (Rochester, VT: Destiny Books, 2015), 131.

2   "Every one of our body's atoms is traceable to the big bang and to the thermonuclear furnaces within high-mass stars that exploded

more than five billion years ago. We are stardust brought to life." Neil deGrasse Tyson, *Astrophysics for People in a Hurry* (New York: W. W. Norton, 2017), 33.

3   "No way around it: some of the water you just drank passed through the kidneys of Socrates, Genghis Kahn, and Joan of Arc. . . . That means some of the air you just breathed passed through the lungs of Napoleon, Beethoven, Lincoln, and Billy the Kid." deGrasse Tyson, *Astrophysics*, 202.

4   Frans de Waal, *Are We Smart Enough to Know How Smart Animals Are?* (New York: W. W. Norton, 2017), 5.

5   de Waal, *Are We Smart*, 76–94, 132–35, 185–201.

6   de Waal, 205–34.

7   Jacqueline Freeman, *Song of Increase: Listening to the Wisdom of Honeybees for Kinder Beekeeping and a Better World* (Boulder, CO: Sounds True, 2016).

8   "If a huge genetic gap separated us from our closest relative in the animal kingdom, we could justifiably celebrate our brilliance. . . . But no such gap exists. Instead, we are one with the rest of nature, fitting neither above nor below, but within." deGrasse Tyson, *Astrophysics*, 201.

CHAPTER 3

1   Carlo Rovelli, *The Order of Time* (New York: Riverhead Books), 2.

2   Rovelli, *Order of Time*, 84.

3   Brian Greene, *The Fabric of the Cosmos: Space, Time, and the Texture of Reality* (New York: Vintage Books, 2004), 453.

4   Eckhart Tolle, *A New Earth: Awakening to Your Life's Purpose* (New York: Plume, 2006), 204.

5   "The light takes time to reach you, let's say a few nanoseconds—a tiny fraction of a second—therefore, you are not quite seeing what she is doing *now* but what she was doing a few nanoseconds ago." Rovelli, *Order of Time*, 41.

6   For a Buddhist perspective on form and formlessness, see Sayadaw U Tejaniya, *When Awareness Becomes Natural: A Guide*

to Cultivating Mindfulness in Everyday Life (Boston: Shambhala, 2016), 58–60.

7   "The elimination of time from your consciousness is the elimination of ego." Tolle, *A New Earth*, 207.

8   Tolle, 207.

CHAPTER 4

1   Neil deGrasse Tyson, *Astrophysics for People in a Hurry* (New York: W. W. Norton, 2017), 203.

2   I discuss some of those experiences in an earlier work, *When Thought Turns to Light: A Practical Guide to Spiritual Transformation* (Rhinebeck, NY: Epigraph, 2016).

3   See Resmaa Menakem, *My Grandmother's Hands: Racialized Trauma and the Pathway to Mending Our Hearts and Bodies* (Las Vegas: Central Recovery, 2017).

4   For an overview of metta with instructions on how to perform it, see Sharon Salzberg, *Loving-kindness: The Revolutionary Art of Happiness* (Boulder, CO: Shambhala, 1995).

CHAPTER 5

1   "Essentialism about identities is usually wrong: in general, there isn't some inner essence that explains why people of a certain social identity are the way they are." Kwame Anthony Appiah, *The Lies that Bind: Rethinking Identity* (New York: Liveright, 2019), 29.

2   "Much of what is dangerous about them has to do with the way identities—religion, nation, race, class, and culture—divide us and set us against one another. They can be enemies of human solidarity." Appiah, *Lies That Bind*, xvi–xvii; "The assertion of an identity always proceeds through contrast or opposition." Appiah, 202.

3   "Many people now know that we are all, in fact, one species, and think that racial differences are, from a biological point of view,

illusory; but that seldom undermines the significance for them of racial identities and affiliations." Appiah, 131.

CHAPTER 6

1   For this reason, people have been drawn to systems like the Enneagram or Human Design that help to illuminate the human mind and to locate themselves in that system. These are roadmaps, designed by others, that can be used as guides or stepping-stones rather than rigid formulas that can aptly capture who you are with a series of questions or an algorithm. Nothing can truly offer a short-cut in figuring out who you are.

2   Mark Nepo, *The Book of Awakening: Having the Life You Want by Being Present to the Life You Have* (Boston: Conari, 2000), 317.

3   Piero Ferrucci, *The Power of Kindness: The Unexpected Benefits of Leading a Compassionate Life* (New York: TarcherPerigree, 2007), 47.

4   David Whyte, *Consolations: The Solace, Nourishment, and Underlying Meaning of Everyday Words* (Langley, WA: Many Rivers Press, 2015), 79.

CHAPTER 7

1   "Our mother has had a unique relationship with us. She has literally made us, and held us inside herself for months. She has nursed, protected, and raised us. She was the first person to love us. At least, that is how it should have been, and how we have always expected it to be." Piero Ferrucci, *The Power of Kindness: The Unexpected Benefits of Leading a Compassionate Life* (New York: TarcherPerigree, 2007), 217.

2   Norman Fischer offers a wonderful take on the need to forgive parents within the Buddhist context. For his formulas for lovingkindness meditation with forgiveness folded in, see *Taking Our Places: The Buddhist Path to Truly Growing Up* (New York: HarperOne, 2003), 92.

3   Fischer, *Taking Our Places*, 97.

4   This is not poetic expression. "Each of us—like any massive object—also warps the spatial fabric in close proximity to our bodies." Brian Greene, *The Elegant Universe: Superstrings, Hidden Dimensions, and the Quest for the Ultimate Theory* (New York: W. W. Norton, 2010), 70–71.

CHAPTER 9

1   Kahlil Gibran, *The Prophet* (New York: Alfred A. Knopf, 1923), 80.

CONCLUSION

1   Brian Greene, *The Elegant Universe: Superstrings, Hidden Dimensions, and the Quest for the Ultimate Theory* (New York: W. W. Norton, 2010), 34–35.

2   "In other words, things that are simultaneous from the viewpoint of some observers will not be simultaneous from the viewpoint of others, if the two groups are in relative motion." Carlo Rovelli, *The Order of Time* (New York: Riverhead Books), 15. "In a physics laboratory, a clock on a table and another on the ground run at different speeds. Which of the two tells the time? There is not 'truer' time; there are two times and they change relative to each other." Greene, *Elegant Universe*, 36.

3   Greene, 3–4, 6.

CPSIA information can be obtained
at www.ICGtesting.com
Printed in the USA
JSHW022131100822
29140JS00002B/6

9 781954 744813